ENGAGED

AN ENTIRELY ORIGINAL FARCICAL

COMEDY IN THREE ACTS

Engaged

An Entirely Original Farcical Comedy in Three Acts

W.S. GILBERT

with notes and an introduction by

Andrew Crowther

SECRETARY OF THE

W.S. GILBERT SOCIETY

RENARD PRESS

RENARD PRESS LTD

Kemp House
152–160 City Road
London EC1V 2NX
United Kingdom
info@renardpress.com
020 8050 2928

www.renardpress.com

Engaged first published in 1877
This edition first published by Renard Press Ltd in 2021

Edited text © Renard Press Ltd, 2021
Introduction, Glossary and Notes © Andrew Crowther, 2021

Cover design by Will Dady

Printed in the United Kingdom by Severn

ISBN: 978-1-913724-42-9

9 8 7 6 5 4 3 2 1

A CIP catalogue record for this book is available from the British Library.

CONTENTS

W.S. GILBERT

A Brief Introduction

William Schwenck Gilbert was born in London on the 18th of November 1836. He was educated at the Western Grammar School, Brompton, and King's College, London. He had intended to go on to complete his education at Oxford, but in the event he was not able to do so, probably for financial reasons. From 1857 to 1862 he was employed by the Education Office as an Assistant Clerk (Third Class) – a job he hated – and he also practised as a barrister between 1863 and about 1867, without much success. He married Lucy Agnes Turner in 1867, their marriage lasting for the rest of his life.

In 1861, a new comic journal called *Fun* appeared, founded in direct imitation of *Punch*. Gilbert began contributing to *Fun* shortly after its first appearance, and for ten years he was one of its most prolific contributors, providing whimsical and comic material of various sorts, including jokes, cartoons, satirical squibs, parody reviews, stories and comic poems. His riotously funny *Bab Ballads*, for a long time considered classic, were first published in *Fun*.

However, his ambition was always to write for the stage. His first acknowledged play, a burlesque called *Dulcamara, or, The Little Duck and the Great Quack*, was a great success when it was produced in 1866. He quickly made a name for himself as a bold and original voice in the theatre, writing all kinds of plays from burlesques and farces to serious dramas. In 1872, an article in *The Era* praised him on the grounds that 'more than all others in our day, he has given us… plays which add to our wealth of dramatic literature; plays which must live.'

In 1871, at the behest of theatrical manager John Hollingshead, Gilbert wrote the libretto for *Thespis*, his first collaboration with composer Arthur Sullivan. It was an ephemeral Christmas entertainment, not expected to have a life beyond its first production, and it was received as such. It was the success of their second comic opera, *Trial by Jury* (1875), that led impresario Richard D'Oyly Carte to consider the commercial possibilities of a longer-term collaboration of Gilbert with Sullivan. Two years later, D'Oyly Carte formed an opera company which, over the next twelve years, would produce ten Gilbert and Sullivan operas, including *HMS Pinafore*, *The Pirates of Penzance*, *Iolanthe*, *The Mikado*, *The Yeomen of the Guard* and *The Gondoliers*. During this time, Gilbert's focus turned more and more towards the Sullivan operas and away from other work.

Over the years, Gilbert's relationship with Sullivan became increasingly strained, due partly to Gilbert's own abrasive personality, and partly to Sullivan's desire to focus on more serious work. In 1890, an explosive business row between Gilbert, D'Oyly Carte and Sullivan fractured the collaboration, though this was later uneasily patched up, leading to two further operas in 1893 and 1896, *Utopia Limited* and *The Grand Duke*.

In 1890 Gilbert moved from his house in Harrington Gardens, South Kensington, to Grim's Dyke, a large country house at Harrow Weald, where he lived for the remainder of his life. In 1897 he went into semi-retirement from the stage, while occasionally writing further plays when the mood came over him. In 1907 he became the first person to be knighted for his achievements as a dramatic author. He died on the 29th of May 1911, suffering from heart failure, having dived into a lake in the grounds of Grim's Dyke, trying to come to the assistance of a young woman who had got into difficulties and called for help.

ANDREW CROWTHER

INTRODUCTION

W.S. Gilbert and

ENGAGED

William Schwenck Gilbert was one of the celebrities of the age. The critic William Archer felt able to declare in his 1882 book *English Dramatists of To-Day*: 'Mr Gladstone is not, Lord Beaconsfield [Benjamin Disraeli] was not, more famous. They have only made the laws of a people – Mr Gilbert has written the songs, and, better still, invented the popular catch-words not of one but two great nations.' This was written in the midst of Gilbert's career, with his most successful work, *The Mikado*, still before him. A few years later, in 1887, Gilbert was able to assert to Sir Arthur Sullivan without too much hyperbole that they were 'as much an institution as Westminster Abbey.'

Today, his main claim to fame is as the wordsmith of the Gilbert and Sullivan operas, but he was also – indeed, as he would have argued, first and foremost – a dramatist in his own right. He wrote over seventy works for the stage, of which the fourteen comic operas with Sullivan form only a small minority. He wrote comedies, farces, 'issue' dramas and tragedies, as well as comic opera libretti for other composers.

Archer called Gilbert 'the most striking individuality, the most original character our theatre of today can boast... in all his work we feel that there is an "awakened" intellect, a thinking brain behind it.' In an age of fast, disposable drama designed for a largely unthinking audience, this characteristic was something of a novelty.

What makes the best of Gilbert's works remain alive to us today is that sense of an ever-lively 'thinking brain' which startles us still with its sharp and merciless humour. In none of his works is it sharper or more merciless than in *Engaged*.

Gilbert's mentor as a dramatist was his older contemporary T.W. (Tom) Robertson (1829–71). In the 1860s, they were colleagues at the comic paper *Fun*. They would attend the first nights of the latest London plays together, discussing and dissecting the pieces afterwards, and they divided between them the responsibility of writing their often scathing reviews for the *Illustrated Times*. It was Robertson who taught Gilbert the importance of directing (or, in the Victorian term, 'stage-managing') one's own plays, and, more vitally, taught him how to do it.

Robertson's plays, if they are remembered today at all, have a reputation for sweet sentimentality; but there is also in them an undertone of critical wit. For example, his 1870 play *M.P.* concludes with the characters speculating what the titular initials might stand for: their suggestions include 'Most Perfidious' and 'Mouth-Patriotism'. Robertson's humour was known to be harsher and more sardonic in person than he let show in his plays. Gilbert's first 'serious' play, *An Old Score* (1869), was clearly indebted to Robertson, though it went much further in its social criticism than Robertson ever dared.

The titles of Robertson's plays – *Society*, *Caste*, *Progress*, *School*, *M.P.*, *War* – suggest an almost didactic intent, though any such intent was never more than intermittently apparent in the plays themselves. The title of Gilbert's *Engaged* recalls Robertson; and perhaps Gilbert was also recalling Robertson's cynical attitude to society during the writing of this, his masterpiece of non-musical drama.

Engaged is, first and foremost, a very funny play, full of crazy situations and barbed wit. At a more 'serious' level, it can be read as a deliberate act of disruption. It takes the conventions of mid-Victorian drama and upends them. In every scene, there is a sense of something awry. The stock figures – noble hero, innocent heroine, evil villain, virtuous peasant, 'good old man' – all find themselves exhibiting strangely changed characteristics and taking on each other's roles, maintaining their usual rhetoric but with altered meanings. The supposed hero, Cheviot Hill, is a mean, lecherous and bad-tempered cad. Belvawney, costumed in the black cloak of a melodramatic villain and bearing a villain's long moustache and dark glasses, turns out to be the nearest thing to a hero that the play can offer. The baby-talking heroine keeps herself surprisingly well informed about stocks and shares; and as for the Good Old Man, he appears to have no redeeming features whatsoever. Every character, even Belvawney, is ultimately shown to be motivated by sheer selfishness and greed. As the French critic Augustin Filon said twenty years later in his book *The English Stage* (1897): 'So cruel a farce had never been seen... The spectators laughed, but the jest was too bitter for their palate. It was at once too unreal and too true.'

The play certainly divided opinion. Its first performance on the 3rd of October 1877 was greeted with 'an outburst of cheers and dissatisfaction', according to a review in *The Echo* on the 10th of October.

The audience's divided response to the play was also reflected in the critical reaction, which has been summarised by Michael R. Booth in his compilation of 'Criticism of *Engaged*' in *English Plays of the Nineteenth Century, III: Comedies* (Oxford: Clarendon Press, 1973). Much of the criticism was remarkably vitriolic, to the extent that one can only surmise a touched nerve. The review in the *Figaro* on the 10th of October 1877 was perhaps the most extreme example:

> To tell the story of *Engaged* is more than can be expected of anyone who assisted at its first representation. One does not care to relate the details of a rough passage across the Channel, if one is not proof against seasickness. The recapitulation of the symptoms of nausea is neither pleasant to

the sufferer, nor edifying to his audience. Let our readers conceive a play in three acts, during which every character only opens his or her mouth to ridicule, in the coarsest manner, every feeling that is generally held in respect by any decent man or woman... From beginning to end of this nauseous play not one of the characters ever says a single word or does a single action that is not inseparable from the lowest moral degradation; while, much to the delight of that portion of the audience who believe that to scoff at what is pure and noble is the surest sign of intellectual pre-eminence, speeches in which the language ordinarily employed by true feeling is used for the purpose of deriding every virtue which any honest man reverences, even if he does not possess, are tediously reiterated by actresses whom one would wish to associate only with what is pure and modest... To answer that 'all this is a burlesque' seems to us but a poor defence; the characters are dressed in the ordinary costume of the present day; the language, as we have said, is precisely that which would be employed in serious drama; there are few if any of those amusing exaggerations which, in true burlesque, dispel, almost before it has time to form, any idea that the speaker is really in earnest. We do not believe that, except among the most repulsive comedies of the seventeenth century, or in the very lowest specimens of French farce, can there be found anything to equal in its heartlessness Mr Gilbert's latest original work.

It's worth noting here that, in the Victorian age, burlesque was different from what we might understand by the term today. It was a kind of theatrical parody, usually in rhymed verse and dotted with songs using the popular tunes current at the time. The humour was of the broadest kind, composed mainly of puns and slapstick.

Other reviews of *Engaged* were almost as scathing, calling it a 'snarling mockery' (*Hornet*, 10th October 1877) and 'a premeditated insult' (*Theatre*, 16th October 1877).

Elsewhere, the critics were more complimentary, though agreeing in regard to its shocking nature. *The Daily Telegraph* (6th October 1877) proclaimed: '[Gilbert] strips off the outward covering concealing our imperfections, and makes us stand shivering. The failings we are aware of, the thoughts we scarcely dare utter are proclaimed to the world and diagnosed by this merciless surgeon.' *The Evening Standard* of the 5th of October 1877 affirmed the play to be 'in many respects one of the most remarkable pieces the stage has produced for many years… *Engaged* satirises with ruthless and scathing sarcasm the selfishness which is so often hidden under the loftiest sentiment…' *The Athenaeum* (13th October 1877) stated with what might be called modified rapture: 'The experiment has rarely, if ever before, been made of supplying a drama in three acts in which there is not a single human being who does not proclaim himself absolutely detestable. In the present instance it has been made, and it is a success.'

However, 'Our Captious Critic' of *The Illustrated Sporting and Dramatic News* of the 20th of October 1877 was somewhat bemused by the whole brouhaha:

It seldom falls to the lot of a comic drama to evoke such diverse critical opinions as have generally been passed upon W.S. Gilbert's new and original piece *Engaged*, at the Haymarket Theatre. The fact that this farcical comedy has had the effect of initiating a certain kind of playgoer into the strongest expressions of condemnation, and of arousing in another kind of spectator the liveliest admiration and eulogy is the surest proof that it is an unique and remarkable production.

For my own part I will say at once that I consider *Engaged* the cleverest comic work that has proceeded from Mr Gilbert's brilliant pen. Having begun by this admission, I must also confess that I have been altogether puzzled by the serious denunciations which have been levelled by critics against what they call the 'heartless cynicism' of one of the most humorous, whimsically incongruous, utterly comical burlesques it has ever been my lot to see or read. Indeed, when some of the critics of *Engaged* deduced from its three acts of grotesque drollery awful evidences of a mind diseased, a lacerated heart, more bitterly sceptical of human good than Dean Swift's *sæva indignatio*,[1] more terrible than his against the human race,

---

[1] *Dean Swift's sæva indignatio*: 'Savage indignation' (Latin); a reference to the epitaph of Jonathan Swift (1667–1745), which he wrote for himself: 'Here lies the body of Jonathan Swift, Doctor of Sacred Theology, Dean of this Cathedral, where savage indignation can no longer injure the heart. Go forth, voyager, and copy, if you can, this vigorous (to the best of his ability) champion of liberty'.

I protest I am fairly mystified. I went and saw the piece a second time, thinking that perchance upon my first visit I might not have sufficiently studied it to apprehend fully the import of its conception and its dialogue. But my impressions remained the same. I had an extra chuckle or so, perhaps, over one or two touches of grave banter that had previously escaped my notice. But after careful consideration of the whole case I was quite unable to regard *Engaged* as anything more serious than a whimsical, satirical, exquisitely humorous extravaganza.

Gilbert did not make a habit of commenting on his own works, except in very practical terms. However, in the case of *Engaged*, there was one particular issue which, he felt, did call for clarification.

As has been mentioned, Gilbert directed the productions of his own plays, in order to ensure that his artistic intent was to some degree conveyed in performance. However, despite all his efforts, he did not always succeed. George Honey, who created the role of Cheviot Hill, played the part in a spirit of broad humour, to Gilbert's fury. 'Honey is simply damnable – self-conscious and extravagant,' he complained in a letter to the actor E.A. Sothern. And so it was that, nine days after the première, Gilbert wrote a short note to be published in the Samuel French acting edition of the play:

It is absolutely essential to the success of this piece that it should be played with the most perfect earnestness and gravity throughout. There should be no exaggeration in costume, make-up or demeanour; and the characters, one and all, should appear to believe, throughout, in the perfect sincerity of their words and actions. Directly the actors show that they are conscious of the absurdity of their utterances the piece begins to drag.

And it is surely no coincidence that the note on costumes also published in the Samuel French edition, and in all likelihood written by Gilbert, stated against Cheviot Hill's name: 'All extravagance of costume in this part should be carefully avoided.'

This insistence on an absence of exaggeration in comic acting was fundamental to Gilbert's method, and there are numerous anecdotes to show that he brought it to his productions of the Gilbert and Sullivan operas. For instance, George Grossmith, creator of many of the patter roles (a staple of comic opera characterised by fast, tongue-twisting text), quoted Gilbert in his 1888 memoir *A Society Clown* as saying: 'I don't want you to *tell* the audience you're the funny man. They'll find it out, if you are, quickly enough.' However, the principle was especially vital in the case of *Engaged*. The play's tone is very finely balanced, and it does not take much to upset that balance in performance.

Towards the end of the following year, 1878, Gilbert wrote a short but powerful essay called 'A Hornpipe in Fetters' for *The Era Almanack* (*The Era* being the weekly paper of the theatrical profession). In it, he argued that there were multiple restrictions on what a British dramatist could write – not through any formal censorship, but because of the increasingly puritanical tastes of the critics who establish the 'dramatic common law'. It was due to them that, for instance, 'no married man... may be in love with anybody but his wife, and, in like manner, no single lady may see any charm in a married man.' But this was not Gilbert's only complaint:

> It has recently been discovered by many dramatic critics that satire and cynicism are misplaced in comedy, and that the propriety of repartee is to be estimated by the standard of conversation in a refined drawing room. It is fortunate for Sheridan that this ukase [decree] had not been pronounced when he wrote *The School for Scandal*; and it is particularly fortunate for M. Victorien Sardou and other French dramatic authors of today that this particular fetter is intended only for the discomfiture of dramatic malefactors of British origin.

While Gilbert was careful to keep his point general and did not mention *Engaged* in particular, it is hard to avoid the feeling that the example of his play was in his mind as he wrote those words.

The original production of *Engaged* lasted for 110 performances – a fairly good run for the time. There were major London revivals in 1881, starring

H.J. Byron as Cheviot Hill, and, in 1886, with a young Herbert Beerbohm Tree in that role.

It seems likely that that Oscar Wilde, rising to fame in London throughout the 1880s, saw *Engaged* during this time, and it is almost certain that he would have read it when it was published in Gilbert's collection *Original Plays: Second Series* in 1881. As many have noted over the years, Wilde's 1895 masterpiece *The Importance of Being Earnest* shows traces of a fruitful study of *Engaged* – not only in some of the details (the donning of mock-mourning, the argument over finger-food, 'Bunburying' versus 'Belvawneying'), but also in tone, which in each case shows a curious coolness of utterance, a strange separation between statement and sincerity. Bernard Shaw, reviewing the first production of *The Importance of Being Earnest* in *The Saturday Review*, was only one of several critics who noticed a similarity with Gilbert, referring disparagingly to 'a scene between the two girls in the second act quite in the literary style of Mr Gilbert, and almost inhuman enough to have been conceived by him.'

Nevertheless, and notwithstanding the specific and general resemblances, Wilde's play has a completely different atmosphere and tone to Gilbert's: light, airy and somehow weightless, where *Engaged*, in spite of all its frivolity, has something serious and even angry behind it. It is a deliberate challenge to the material-istic values of its time:

SYMPERSON: This is a pretty business! Done out of a thousand a year, and by my own daughter! What a terrible thing is this incessant craving after money! Upon my word, some people seem to think that they're sent into the world for no other purpose but to acquire wealth, and, by Jove, they'll sacrifice their nearest and dearest relations to get it.

The difference between the two plays can also be seen their contrasting fates: *The Importance of Being Earnest* quickly emerged as an evergreen favourite of audiences, while *Engaged* has always been seen as a 'problem'. For much of the twentieth century, *Engaged* lay neglected, if not quite ignored, and almost untouched by the professional theatre. Like Gilbert's other non-musical works, its reputation has been eclipsed by the worldwide success of the Gilbert and Sullivan operas. The general verdict of the public and the critics may be summarised by William Archer's 1882 observation that 'Mr Sullivan's music appears to have the power of soothing [Gilbert's] savage breast, and sweetening the gall and bitterness which flavour such a play as *Engaged*.'

A notable exception to the neglect of *Engaged* was the National Theatre's 1975 production of the play with a stellar case including Jonathan Pryce, David Egan and Pauline Collins. More recently, there have been major productions at the Orange Tree Theatre in Richmond upon Thames (2002), the Lucille Lortel Theatre in New York (2004), the Pitlochry Festival Theatre in Scotland (2004) and the Royal George Theatre in Ontario, as part of the annual Shaw Festival (2016). These and other stagings have helped to demonstrate to modern audiences the play's brilliance in the theatre as well as on the page.

But in the end, after all the debates about the play's morality, truth, cynicism, ability to hold the stage and so on, the essence of its value remains in its sheer gleeful *funniness*, as William Archer recognised when he called it 'a repulsive, vulgar and – extremely amusing play.'

ANDREW CROWTHER

ENGAGED

*An entirely original farcical
comedy in three acts*

DRAMATIS PERSONAE

CHEVIOT HILL,* *a young man of property*
BELVAWNEY, *his friend*
MR SYMPERSON
ANGUS MACALISTER,* *a Lowland peasant lad*
MAJOR MCGILLICUDDY
BELINDA TREHERNE, 'MISS TREHERNE'
MINNIE, SYMPERSON*'s daughter*
MRS MACFARLANE, *a Lowland widow*
MAGGIE, *her daughter, a Lowland lassie*
PARKER, MINNIE*'s maid*

COSTUMES

CHEVIOT HILL, *suit of dittos.**
All extravagance of costume in this part
should be carefully avoided.
BELVAWNEY, *black frock coat and trousers, black tie,*
simple black cloak, long black wig and moustache,
pale face, green spectacles.
MR SYMPERSON, *morning dress.*
ANGUS MACALISTER, *Scotch peasant, short coat,*
knee breeches, woollen stockings, glengarry,*
plaid over shoulder.

3

MAJOR MCGILLICUDDY, *frock coat, white waistcoat,
grey trousers, wedding favour.*
BELINDA TREHERNE, *aesthetic walking dress
in Act I; deep black in Act II;
morning dress in Act III.*
MINNIE, *wedding dress in Act II;
morning dress in Act III.*
MRS MACFARLANE, *Scotch peasant woman, short
jacket, ankle homespun petticoat, white nightcap.*
MAGGIE, *Scotch peasant girl, short skirt,
grey stockings, snood.**
PARKER, *as a ladies' maid.*

SETTING

ACT I
*Garden of a cottage near Gretna**
(on the border between England and Scotland).

ACTS II AND III
Drawing room in SYMPERSON'*s house in London.*

*Three months' interval is supposed to elapse
between acts I and II.*

*Three days' interval is supposed to elapse
between acts II and III.*

4

NOTE

It is absolutely essential to the success of this piece that it should be played with the most perfect earnestness and gravity throughout. There should be no exaggeration in costume, make-up or demeanour; and the characters, one and all, should appear to believe, throughout, in the perfect sincerity of their words and actions. Directly the actors show that they are conscious of the absurdity of their utterances the piece begins to drag.

W.S. GILBERT.
24, The Boltons*
12th October, 1877

ACT I

SCENE

Garden of a humble but picturesque cottage near Gretna, on the border between England and Scotland. The whole scene is suggestive of rustic prosperity and content. MAGGIE MACFARLANE, *a pretty country girl, is discovered spinning at a wheel, and singing as she spins.* ANGUS MACALISTER, *a good-looking peasant lad, appears on at back, and creeps softly down to* MAGGIE *as she sings and spins, and places his hands over her eyes.*

ANGUS: Wha is it?
MAGGIE: Oh, Angus, ye frightened me sae!

(*He releases her.*)

    And see there – the flax is a' knotted and scribbled – and I'll do naething wi' it!
ANGUS: Meg! My Meg! My ain bonnie Meg!
MAGGIE: Angus, why, lad, what's wrang wi' ee? Thou hast teardrops in thy bonnie blue een.
ANGUS: Dinna heed them, Meg. It comes fra glowerin' at thy bright beauty. Glowerin' at thee is like glowerin' at the noonday sun!
MAGGIE: Angus, thou'rt talking fulishly. I'm but a puir brown hillside lassie. I dinna like to hear sic things

from a straight honest lad like thee. It's the way the dandy tounfolk speak to me, and it does na come rightly from the lips of a simple man.

ANGUS: Forgive me, Meg, for I speak honestly to ye. Angus Macalister is not the man to deal in squeaming compliments. Meg, I love thee dearly, as thou well knowest. I'm but a puir lad, and I've little but twa braw arms and a straight hairt to live by, but I've saved a wee bit siller – I've a braw housie and a scrappie of gude garden land – and it's a' for thee, lassie, if thou'll gie me thy true and tender little hairt!

MAGGIE: Angus, I'll be fair and straight wi' ee. Thou askest me for my hairt. Why, Angus, thou'rt tall, and fair, and brave. Thou'st a gude, honest face, and a gude, honest hairt, which is mair precious than a' the gold on earth! No man has a word to say against Angus Macalister – no, nor any woman, neither. Thou hast strong arms to work wi', and a strong hairt to help thee work. And wha am I that I should say that a' these blessings are not enough for me? If thou, gude, brave, honest man, will be troubled wi' sic a puir little humble mousie as Maggie Macfarlane, why, she'll just be the proudest and happiest lassie in a' Dumfries!*

ANGUS: My ain darling!

(*They embrace. Enter* MRS MACFARLANE *from cottage.*)

MRS MACFARLANE: Why, Angus, Maggie, what's a' this!

ANGUS: Mistress Macfarlane, dinna be fasht wi' me; dinna think worse o' me than I deserve. I've loved your lass honestly these fifteen years, but I never plucked up the hairt to tell her so until noo; and when she answered fairly, it wasna in human nature to do aught else but hold her to my hairt and place one kiss on her bonnie cheek.

MRS MACFARLANE: Angus, say nae mair. My hairt is sair at losing my only bairn; but I'm nae fasht wi' ee. Thou'rt a gude lad, and it's been the hope of my widowed auld heart to see you twain one. Thou'lt treat her kindly – I ken that weel. Thou'rt a prosperous, kirk-going man, and my Mag should be a happy lass indeed. Bless thee, Angus, bless thee!

ANGUS (*wiping his eyes*): Dinna heed the water in my ee – it will come when I'm ower glad. Yes, I'm a fairly prosperous man. What wi' farmin' a bit land, and gillieing* odd times, and a bit o' poachin' now and again; and what wi' my illicit whusky still – and throwin' trains off the line, that the poor distracted passengers may come to my cot,* I've mair ways than one of making an honest living – and I'll work them a' nicht and day for my bonnie Meg!

MRS MACFARLANE: D'ye ken, Angus, I sometimes think that thou'rt losing some o' thine auld skill at upsetting railway trains. Thou hast not done sic a thing these sax weeks, and the cottage stands sairly in need of sic chance custom as the poor delayed passengers may bring.

MAGGIE: Nay, Mither, thou wrangest him. Even noo, this very day, has he not placed twa bonnie braw sleepers across the up-line, ready for the express from Glaisgie, which is due in twa minutes or so?

MRS MACFARLANE: Gude lad! Gude thoughtfu' lad! But I hope the unfortunate passengers will na' be much hurt, puir unconscious bodies!

ANGUS: Fear nought, Mither. Lang experience has taught me to do my work deftly. The train will run off the line, and the traffic will just be blocked for half a day, but I'll warrant ye that, wi' a' this, nae mon, woman or child amang them will get sae much as a bruised head or a broken nose.

MAGGIE: My ain tender-hearted Angus! He wadna hurt sae much as a blatherin' buzzin' bluebottle flee!

ANGUS: Nae, Meg, not if takin' care and thought could help the poor dumb thing! (*Wiping his eyes:*) There, see, lass (*looking off*), the train's at a standstill, and there's nae harm done. I'll just go and tell the puir distraught passengers that they may rest them here, in thy cot, gin they will, till the line is cleared again. Mither, get thy rooms ready, and put brose i' the pot, for mebbe they'll be hungry, puir souls. Farewell, Meg; I'll be back ere lang, and if I don't bring ee a full half dozen o' well-paying passengers, thou may'st just wed the redheaded exciseman! (*Exit.*)

MAGGIE: Oh, Mither, Mither, I'm ower happy! I've nae deserved sic a good fortune as to be the wife o' yon brave and honest lad!

MRS MACFARLANE: Meg, thine auld mither's hairt is sair at the thought o' losin' ye, for hitherto she's just been a' the world to ee, but now thou'lt cleave to thine Angus, and thou'lt learn to love him better than thy puir auld mither! But it mun be – it mun be!

MAGGIE: Nay, Mither, say not that. A gude girl loves her husband wi' one love and her mither wi' anither. They are not alike, but neither is greater nor less than the ither, and they dwell together in peace and unity. That is how a gude girl loves.

MRS MACFARLANE: And thou art a gude girl, Meg?

MAGGIE: I am a varra gude girl indeed, Mither – a varra, varra gude girl!

MRS MACFARLANE: I'm richt sure o' that. Well, the puir belated passengers will be here directly, and it is our duty to provide for them sic puir hospitality as our humble roof will afford. It shall never be said o' Janie Macfarlane that she ever turned the weary traveller fainting from her door.

MAGGIE: My ain gentle-hearted mither!

(*Exeunt together into cottage. Enter* ANGUS *with* BELVAWNEY *and* MISS TREHERNE. *She is in travelling costume, and both are much agitated and alarmed.*)

ANGUS: Step in, sir – step in, and sit ye doun for a wee. I'll just send Mistress Macfarlane to ye. She's a gude auld bodie, and will see to your comforts as if she was your ain mither.

BELVAWNEY: Thank you, my worthy lad, for your kindness at this trying moment. I assure you we shall not forget it.

ANGUS: Ah, sir, wadna any mon do as muckle? A dry shelter, a bannock and a pan o' parritch is a' we can offer ye, but sic as it is ye're hairtily welcome.

BELVAWNEY: It is well – we thank you.

ANGUS: For wha wadna help the unfortunate?

BELVAWNEY (*occupied with* MISS TREHERNE): Exactly –
  everyone would.

ANGUS: Or feed the hungry?

BELVAWNEY: No doubt.

ANGUS: It just brings the tear drop to my ee to think—

BELVAWNEY (*leading him off*): My friend, we would be
  alone, this maiden and I. Farewell!

(*Exit* ANGUS *into cottage.*)

  Belinda – my own – my life! Compose yourself. It was
  in truth a weird and gruesome accident. The line is
  blocked, your parasol is broken and your butterscotch
  trampled in the dust, but no serious harm is done.
  Come, be cheerful. We are safe – quite safe.

MISS TREHERNE: Safe! Ah, Belvawney, my own, own
  Belvawney – there is, I fear, no safety for us so long
  as we are liable to be overtaken by that fearful Major
  to whom I was to have been married this morning!

BELVAWNEY: Major McGillicuddy? I confess I do not feel
  comfortable when I think of Major McGillicuddy.

MISS TREHERNE: You know his barbaric nature, and
  how madly jealous he is. If he should find that I
  have eloped with you, he will most surely shoot us
  both!

BELVAWNEY: It is an uneasy prospect. (*Suddenly:*) Belinda,
  do you love me?

MISS TREHERNE: With an impetuous passion that I shall
  carry with me to the tomb!

BELVAWNEY: Then be mine tomorrow! We are not far
  from Gretna, and the thing can be done without

delay. Once married, the arm of the law will protect us from this fearful man, and we can defy him to do his worst.

MISS TREHERNE: Belvawney, all this is quite true. I love you madly, passionately; I care to live but in your heart; I breathe but for your love; yet, before I actually consent to take the irrevocable step that will place me on the pinnacle of my fondest hopes, you must give me some definite idea of your pecuniary position. I am not mercenary, Heaven knows; but business is business, and I confess I should like a little definite information about the settlements.

BELVAWNEY: I often think that it is deeply to be deplored that these grovelling questions of money should alloy the tenderest and most hallowed sentiments that inspire our imperfect natures.

MISS TREHERNE: It is unfortunate, no doubt, but at the same time it is absolutely necessary.

BELVAWNEY: Belinda, I will be frank with you. My income is £1000 a year, which I hold on certain conditions. You know my friend Cheviot Hill, who is travelling to London in the same train with us, but in the third class?

MISS TREHERNE: I believe I know the man you mean.

BELVAWNEY: Cheviot, who is a young man of large property, but extremely close-fisted, is cursed with a strangely amatory disposition, as you will admit when I tell you that he has contracted a habit of proposing marriage, as a matter of course, to every woman he meets. His haughty father (who comes of a very old family – the Cheviot Hills had settled in this part of

the world centuries before the Conquest) is compelled
by his health to reside in Madeira. Knowing that I
exercise an all but supernatural influence over his
son, and fearing that his affectionate disposition
would lead him to contract an undesirable marriage,
the old gentleman allows me £1000 a year so long as
Cheviot shall live single, but at his death or marriage
the money goes over to Cheviot's uncle Symperson,
who is now travelling to town with him.

MISS TREHERNE: Then so long as your influence over
him lasts, so long only will you retain your income?

BELVAWNEY: That is, I am sorry to say, the state of the
case.

MISS TREHERNE (*after a pause*): Belvawney, I love you
with an imperishable ardour which mocks the power
of words. If I were to begin to tell you now of the
force of my indomitable passion for you, the tomb
would close over me before I could exhaust the
entrancing subject. But, as I said before, business is
business, and unless I can see some distinct probabil-
ity that your income will be permanent, I shall have
no alternative but to weep my heart out in all the
anguish of maiden solitude – uncared for, unloved
and alone! (*Exit into cottage.*)

BELVAWNEY: There goes a noble-hearted girl, indeed!
Oh, for the gift of Cheviot's airy badinage – oh,
for his skill in weaving a net about the hearts of
women! If I could but induce her to marry me at
once before the dreadful Major learns our flight!
Why not? We are in Scotland. Methinks I've heard
two loving hearts can wed in this strange country by

merely making declaration to that effect. I will think out some cunning scheme to lure her into marriage unawares.

(*Enter* MAGGIE *from cottage.*)

MAGGIE: Will ye walk in and rest a wee, Maister Belvawney? There's a room ready for ye, kind sir, and ye're heartily welcome to it.

BELVAWNEY: It is well. Stop! Come hither, maiden.

MAGGIE: Oh, sir! You do not mean any harm towards a puir, innocent, unprotected cottage lassie?

BELVAWNEY: Harm! No, of course I don't. What do you mean?

MAGGIE: I'm but a puir humble mountain girl; but let me tell you, sir, that my character's just as dear to me as the richest and proudest lady's in the land. Before I consent to approach ye, swear to me that you mean me no harm.

BELVAWNEY: Harm? Of course I don't. Don't be a little fool. Come here.

MAGGIE (*aside*): There is something in his manner that reassures me. It is not that of the airy trifler with innocent hairts. —What wad ye wi' puir harmless Maggie MacFarlane, gude sir?

BELVAWNEY: Can you tell me what constitutes a Scotch marriage?*

MAGGIE: Oh, sir, it's nae use asking me that; for my hairt is not my ain to give. I'm betrothed to the best and noblest lad in a' the bonnie Borderland. Oh, sir, I canna be your bride!

BELVAWNEY: My girl, you mistake. I do not want you for my bride. Can't you answer a simple question? What constitutes a Scotch marriage?

MAGGIE: Ye've just to say before twa witnesses, 'Maggie Macfarlane is my wife', and I've just to say, 'Maister Belvawney is my husband', and nae mon can set us asunder. But, sir, I canna be your bride; for I am betrothed to the best and noblest—

BELVAWNEY: I congratulate you. You can go.

MAGGIE: Yes, sir. (*Exit into cottage.*)

BELVAWNEY: It is a simple process – simple, but yet how beautiful! One thing is certain – Cheviot may marry any day, despite my precautions, and then I shall be penniless. He may die, and equally I shall be penniless. Belinda has £500 a year; it is not much, but it would, at least, save me from starvation.

(*Exit* BELVAWNEY. *Enter* SYMPERSON *and* CHEVIOT HILL *over bridge. They both show signs of damage – their hats are beaten in and their clothes disordered through the accident.*)

SYMPERSON: Well, here we are at last—

CHEVIOT: Yes; here we are at last, and a pretty state I'm in, to be sure.

SYMPERSON: My dear nephew, you would travel third class, and this is the consequence. After all, there's not much harm done.

CHEVIOT: Not much harm? What d'ye call that? (*Showing his hat.*) Ten and ninepence at one operation! My gloves split – one and four! My coat ruined – eighteen and six! It's a coarse and brutal nature that recognises no harm that don't involve loss of blood. I'm reduced by this accident from a thinking, feeling, reflecting human being, to a moral pulp – a mash, a poultice. Damme, sir, that's what I am! I'm a poultice!

SYMPERSON: Cheviot, my dear boy, at the moment of the accident you were speaking to me on a very interesting subject.

CHEVIOT: Was I? I forget what it was. The accident has knocked it clean out of my head.

SYMPERSON: You were saying that you were a man of good position and fortune; that you derived £2000 a year from your bank; that you thought it was time you settled. You then reminded me that I should come into Belvawney's £1000 a year on your marriage, and I'm not sure, but I rather think you mentioned, casually, that my daughter Minnie is an angel of light.

CHEVIOT: True, and just then we went off the line. To resume: Uncle Symperson, your daughter Minnie is an angel of light, a perfect being, as innocent as a new-laid egg.

SYMPERSON: Minnie is, indeed, all that you have described her.

CHEVIOT: Uncle, I'm a man of few words. I feel and I speak. I love that girl madly, passionately, irresistibly. She is my whole life, my whole soul and body, my Past, my Present and my To Come. I have thought for none but her; she fills my mind, sleeping and waking; she is the essence of every hope – the tree upon which the fruit of my heart is growing – my own To Come!

SYMPERSON (*who has sunk overpowered on to stool during this speech*): Cheviot, my dear boy, excuse a father's tears.

I won't beat about the bush. You have anticipated my devoutest wish. Cheviot, my dear boy, take her – she is yours!

CHEVIOT: I have often heard of rapture, but I never knew what it was till now. Uncle Symperson, bearing in mind the fact that your income will date from the day of the wedding, when may this be?

SYMPERSON: My boy, the sooner the better! Delicacy would prompt me to give Belvawney a reasonable notice of the impending loss of his income, but should I, for such a mere selfish reason as that, rob my child of one hour of the happiness that you are about to confer upon her? No! Duty to my child is paramount!

CHEVIOT: On one condition, however, I must insist. This must be kept from Belvawney's knowledge. You know the strange, mysterious influence that his dreadful eyes exercise over me.

SYMPERSON: I have remarked* it with astonishment.

CHEVIOT: They are much inflamed just now, and he has to wear green spectacles. While this lasts I am a free agent, but under treatment they may recover. In that case, if he knew that I contemplated matrimony, he would use them to prevent my doing so – and I cannot resist them – I cannot resist them! Therefore, I say, until I am safely and securely tied up, Belvawney must know nothing about it.

SYMPERSON: Trust me, Cheviot, he shall know nothing about it from *me*. (*Aside:*) A thousand a year! I have endeavoured, but in vain, to woo Fortune for fifty-six years, but she smiles upon me at last! She smiles upon me at last! (*Exit into cottage.*)

CHEVIOT: At length my hopes are to be crowned! Oh, my own – my own – the hope of my heart – my love – my life!

(*Enter* BELVAWNEY, *who has overheard these words.*)

BELVAWNEY: Cheviot! Whom are you apostrophising* in those terms? You've been at it again, I see!

CHEVIOT: Belvawney, that apostrophe was private; I decline to admit you to my confidence.

BELVAWNEY: Cheviot, what is the reason of this strange tone of defiance? A week ago I had but to express a wish to have it obeyed as a matter of course.

CHEVIOT: Belvawney, it may not be denied that there was a time when, owing to the remarkable influence exercised over me by your extraordinary eyes, you could do with me as you would. It would be affectation to deny it; your eyes withered my will; they paralysed my volition. They were strange and lurid eyes, and I bowed to them. Those eyes were my Fate – my Destiny – my unerring Must – my inevitable Shall. That time has gone – for ever!

BELVAWNEY: Alas for the days that are past and the good that came and went with them!

CHEVIOT: Weep for them if you will. I cannot weep with you, for I loved them not. But, as you say, they are past. The light that lit up those eyes is extinct – their fire has died out – their soul has fled. They are no longer eyes, they are poached eggs. I have not yet sunk so low as to be the slave of two poached eggs.

BELVAWNEY: Have mercy. If any girl has succeeded in enslaving you – and I know how easily you are enslaved

– dismiss her from your thoughts; have no more to say to her; and I will – yes, I will bless you with my latest breath!*

CHEVIOT: Whether a blessing conferred with one's latest breath is a superior article to one conferred in robust health we need not stop to enquire. I decline, as I said before, to admit you to my confidence on any terms whatever. Begone!

(*Exit* BELVAWNEY.)

Dismiss from my thoughts the only woman I ever loved! Have no more to say to the tree upon which the fruit of my heart is growing! No, Belvawney, I cannot cut off my tree as if it were gas or water. I do not treat women like that. Some men do, but I don't. I am not that sort of man. I respect women; I love women. They are good; they are pure; they are beautiful; at least, many of them are.

(*Enter* MAGGIE *from cottage: he is much fascinated.*)

This one, for example, is very beautiful indeed!

MAGGIE: If ye'll just walk in, sir, ye'll find a bannock and a pan o' parritch waitin' for ye on the table.

CHEVIOT: This is one of the loveliest women I ever met in the whole course of my life!

MAGGIE (*aside*): What's he glowerin' at? —Oh, sir, ye mean no harm to the poor Lowland lassie?

CHEVIOT: Pardon me; it's very foolish. I can't account for it – but I am arrested, fascinated.

22

MAGGIE: Oh, gude sir, what's fascinated ye?

CHEVIOT: I don't know; there is something about you that exercises a most remarkable influence over me; it seems to weave a kind of enchantment around me. I can't think what it is. You are a good girl, I am sure. None but a good girl could so powerfully affect me. You *are* a good girl, are you not?

MAGGIE: I am a varra gude girl indeed, sir.

CHEVIOT: I was quite sure of it. (*Gets his arm round her waist.*)

MAGGIE: I am a much better girl than nineteen out of twenty in these pairts. And they are all gude girls too.

CHEVIOT: My darling! (*Kisses her.*)

MAGGIE: Oh, kind sir, what's that for?

CHEVIOT: It is your reward for being a good girl.

MAGGIE: Oh, sir, I did na look for sic a recompense; you are varra varra kind to puir little Maggie Macfarlane.

CHEVIOT: I cannot think what it is about you that fascinates me so remarkably.

MAGGIE: Maybe it's my beauty.

CHEVIOT: Maybe it is. It is quite possible that it may be, as you say, your beauty.

MAGGIE: I am remarkably pretty, and I've a varra neat figure.

CHEVIOT: There is a natural modesty in this guileless appreciation of your own perfection that is, to me, infinitely more charming than the affected ignorance of an artificial town-bred beauty.

MAGGIE: Oh, sir, can I close my een to the picture that my looking-glass holds up to me twenty times a day? We see the rose on the tree, and we say that it is fair; we see the silver moon sailing in the braw blue heavens, and we say that she is bright; we see the brawling stream purling over the smooth stanes i' the burn, and we say that it is beautiful; and shall we close our een to the fairest of nature's works – a pure and beautiful woman? Why, sir, it wad just be base ingratitude! No, it's best to tell the truth about a' things: I am a varra, varra beautiful girl!

CHEVIOT: Maggie MacFarlane, I'm a plain, blunt, straightforward man, and I come quickly to the point. I see more to love in you than I ever saw in any woman in all my life before. I have a large income, which I do not spend recklessly. I love you passionately; you are the essence of every hope; you are the tree upon which the fruit of my heart is growing – my Past, my Present, my Future – you are my own To Come. Tell me, will you be mine – will you join your life with mine?

(*Enter* ANGUS, *who listens.*)

MAGGIE: Ah, kind sir, I'm sairly grieved to wound sae true and tender a love as yours, but ye're ower late – my love is nae my ain to give ye, it's given ower to the best and bravest lad in a' the bonnie Borderland!

CHEVIOT: Give me his address that I may go and curse him!

MAGGIE (*kneels to* CHEVIOT): Ah, ye must not curse him. Oh, spare him, spare him, for he is good and brave, and he loves me, oh, sae dearly, and I love him, oh, sae dearly too. Oh, sir, kind sir, have mercy on him, and do not (*throwing herself at his feet*) – do not curse him, or I shall die!

CHEVIOT: Will you, or will you not, oblige me by telling me where he is, that I may at once go and curse him?

ANGUS (*coming forward*): He is here, sir, but dinna waste your curses on me. Maggie, my bairn (*raising her*), I heard the answer ye gave to this man, my true and gentle lassie! Ye spake well and bravely, Meg – well and bravely! Dinna heed the water in my ee – it's a tear of joy and gratitude, Meg – a tear of joy and gratitude!

CHEVIOT (*touched, aside*): Poor fellow! I will *not* curse him! —Young man, I respect your honest emotion. I don't want to distress you, but I cannot help loving this most charming girl. Come, is it reasonable to quarrel with a man because he's of the same way of thinking as yourself?

ANGUS: Nay, sir, I'm nae fasht, but it just seems to drive a' the bluid back into my hairt when I think that my Meg is loved by anither! Oh, sir, she's a fair and winsome lassie, and I micht as justly be angry wi' ye for loving the blue heavens! She's just as far above us as they are! (*Wiping his eyes and kissing her.*)

CHEVIOT (*with decision*): Pardon me, I cannot allow that.

ANGUS: Eh?

CHEVIOT: I love that girl madly – passionately – and I cannot possibly allow you to do that – not before my eyes, I beg. You simply torture me.

MAGGIE (*to* ANGUS): Leave off, dear, till the puir gentleman's gone, and then ye can begin again.

CHEVIOT: Angus, listen to me. You love this girl?

ANGUS: I love her, sir, a'most as weel as I love mysel'!

CHEVIOT: Then reflect how you are standing in the way of her prosperity. I am a rich man. I have money, position and education. I am a much more intellectual and generally agreeable companion for her than you can ever hope to be. I am full of anecdote, and all my anecdotes are in the best possible taste. I will tell you some of them some of these days, and you can judge for yourself. Maggie, if she married me, would live in a nice house in a good square. She would have wine – occasionally. She would be kept beautifully clean. Now, if you really love this girl almost as well as you love yourself, are you doing wisely or kindly in standing in the way of her getting all these good things? As to compensation – why, I've had heavy expenses of late, but if – yes, if thirty shillings—

ANGUS (*hotly*): Sir, I'm puir in pocket, but I've a rich hairt. It is rich in a pure and overflowing love, and he that hath love hath all. You canna ken what true love is, or you wadna dare to insult a puir but honest lad by offering to buy his treasure for money.

(CHEVIOT *retires up.*)

MAGGIE: My ain true darling!

(*They embrace.*)

CHEVIOT: Now, I'll not have it! Understand me, I'll not have it. It's simple agony to me. Angus, I respect your indignation, but you are too hasty. I do not offer to buy your treasure for money. You love her; it will naturally cause you pain to part with her, and I prescribe thirty shillings not as a cure, but as a temporary solace. If thirty shillings is not enough, why, I don't mind making it two pounds.

ANGUS: Nae, sir, it's useless, and we ken it weel, do we not, my brave lassie? Our hearts are one as our bodies will be some day; and the man is na born, and the gold is na coined, that can set us twain asunder!

MAGGIE: Angus, dear, I'm varra proud o' sae staunch and true a love; it's like your ain true self, an' I can say nae more for it than that. But dinna act wi'out prudence and forethought, dear. In these hard times twa pound is twa pound, and I'm nae sure that ye're acting richtly in refusing sae large a sum. I love you varra dearly – ye ken that right weel – an' if ye'll be troubled wi' sic a poor little mousie I'll mak' ye a true an' loving wife, but I doubt whether, wi' a' my love, I'll ever be worth as much to ye as twa pound. Dinna act in haste, dear; tak' time to think before ye refuse this kind gentleman's offer.

ANGUS: Oh, sir, is not this rare modesty? Could ye match it amang your toun-bred fine ladies? I think not! Meg, it shall be as you say. I'll tak' the siller, but it'll be wi' a sair and broken hairt!

(CHEVIOT *gives* ANGUS *money.*)

Fare thee weel, my love – my childhood's – boyhood's – manhood's love! Ye're ganging fra my hairt to anither, who'll gie thee mair o' the gude things o' this world than I could ever gie ee, except love, an' o' that my hairt is full indeed! But it's a' for the best; ye'll be happier wi' him – and twa pound is twa pound. Meg, mak' him a gude wife, be true to him and love him as ye loved me. Oh, Meg, my poor bruised hairt is well nigh like to break! (*Exit into cottage, in great agony.*)

MAGGIE (*looking wistfully after him*): Puir laddie, puir laddie! Oh, I did na ken till noo how weel he loved me!

CHEVIOT: Maggie, I'm almost sorry I— Poor lad, poor fellow! He has a generous heart. I am glad I did not curse him. (*Aside:*) This is weakness! —Maggie, my own – ever and for always my own, we will be very happy, will we not?

MAGGIE: Oh, sir, I dinna ken, but in truth I hope so. Oh, sir, my happiness is in your hands noo; be kind to the puir cottage lassie who loves ye sae weel; my hairt is a' your ain, and if ye forsake me my lot will be a sair one indeed! (*Exit, weeping, into cottage.*)

CHEVIOT: Poor little Lowland lassie! That's my idea of a wife. No ridiculous extravagance; no expensive tastes. Knows how to dress like a lady on £5 a year; ah, and does it, too! No pretence there of being blind to her own beauties; she knows that she is beautiful, and scorns to lie about it. In that respect she resembles Symperson's dear daughter, Minnie. My darling Minnie! (*Looks at miniature.*) My own darling Minnie. Minnie is fair, Maggie is dark. Maggie loves me! That excellent and perfect country creature loves me! She is to be the light of my life, my own To Come! In some respects she is even prettier than Minnie – my darling Minnie, Symperson's dear daughter, the tree upon which the

28

fruit of my heart is growing; my Past, my Present and my Future, my own To Come! But this tendency to reverie is growing on me; I must shake it off.

(*Enter* MISS TREHERNE.)

Heaven and earth, what a singularly lovely girl!

MISS TREHERNE: A stranger! Pardon me, I will withdraw!

CHEVIOT: A stranger indeed, in one sense, inasmuch as he never had the happiness of meeting you before – but, in that he has a heart that can sympathise with another's misfortune, he trusts he may claim to be regarded almost as a friend.

MISS TREHERNE: May I ask, sir, to what misfortunes you allude?

CHEVIOT: I – a – do not know their precise nature, but that perception would indeed be dull, and that heart would be indeed flinty, that did not at once perceive that you are very, very unhappy. Accept, madam, my deepest and most respectful sympathy.

MISS TREHERNE: You have guessed rightly, sir! I am indeed a most unhappy woman.

CHEVIOT: I am delighted to hear it – a – I mean, I feel a pleasure, a melancholy and chastened pleasure, in reflecting that, if your distress is not of a pecuniary nature, it may perchance lie in my power to alleviate your sorrow.

MISS TREHERNE: Impossible, sir, though I thank you for your respectful sympathy.

CHEVIOT: How many women would forgo twenty years of their lives to be as beautiful as yourself, little dreaming that extraordinary loveliness can coexist with the most poignant anguish of mind? But so, too often, we find it, do we not, dear lady?

MISS TREHERNE: Sir! This tone of address... from a complete stranger!

CHEVIOT: Nay, be not unreasonably severe upon an impassionable and impulsive man, whose tongue is but the too-faithful herald of his heart. We see the rose on the tree, and we say that it is fair; we see the bonnie brooks purling over the smooth stanes – I should say 'stones' – in the burn, and we say that it is beautiful, and shall we close our eyes to the fairest of nature's works – a pure and beautiful woman? Why, it would be base ingratitude, indeed!

MISS TREHERNE: I cannot deny that there is much truth in the sentiments you so beautifully express, but I am, unhappily, too well aware that, whatever advantages I may possess, personal beauty is not among their number.

CHEVIOT: How exquisitely modest is this chaste insensibility to your own singular loveliness! How infinitely more winning than the bold-faced self-appreciation of under-bred country girls!

MISS TREHERNE: I am glad, sir, that you are pleased with my modesty. It has often been admired.

CHEVIOT: Pleased! I am more than pleased – that's a very weak word. I am enchanted. Madam, I am a man of quick impulse and energetic action. I feel and I speak – I cannot help it. Madam, be not surprised when I tell you that I cannot resist the conviction that you are the light of my future life, the essence of every hope, the tree upon which the fruit of my heart is growing – my Past, my Present, my Future, my own To Come! Do not extinguish that light, do not disperse that essence, do not blight that tree! I am well off; I'm a bachelor; I'm thirty-two; and I love you, madam, humbly, truly, trustfully, patiently. Paralysed with admiration, I wait anxiously, and yet hopefully, for your reply.

MISS TREHERNE: Sir, that heart would indeed be cold that did not feel grateful for so much earnest, single-hearted devotion. I am deeply grieved to have to say one word to cause pain to one who expresses himself in such well-chosen terms of respectful esteem; but, alas! I have already yielded up my heart to one who, if I mistake not, is a dear personal friend of your own.

CHEVIOT: Am I to understand that you are the young lady of property whom Belvawney hopes to marry?

MISS TREHERNE: I am, indeed, that unhappy woman!

CHEVIOT: And is it possible that you love him?

MISS TREHERNE: With a rapture that thrills every fibre of my heart – with a devotion that enthralls my very soul! But there's some difficulty about his settlements.

CHEVIOT: A difficulty! I should think there was. Why, on my marrying, his entire income goes over to Symperson! I could reduce him to penury tomorrow. As it happens, I *am* engaged, I recollect, to Symperson's daughter; and if Belvawney dares to interpose between you and me, by George, I'll do it!

MISS TREHERNE: Oh, spare him, sir! You say that you love me? Then, for my sake, remain single for ever – it is all I ask, it is not much. Promise me that you will never, never marry, and we will both bless you with our latest breath!

CHEVIOT: There seems to be a special importance attached to a blessing conferred with one's latest breath that I entirely fail to grasp. It seems to me to convey no definite advantage of any kind whatever.

MISS TREHERNE: Cruel, cruel man!

(*Enter* BELVAWNEY, *in great alarm.*)

BELVAWNEY: We are lost! We are lost!

MISS TREHERNE: What do you mean?

CHEVIOT: Who has lost you?

BELVAWNEY: Major McGillicuddy discovered your flight, and followed in the next train. The line is blocked through our accident, and his train has pulled up within a few yards of our own. He is now making his way to this very cottage! What do you say to that?

MISS TREHERNE: I agree with you – we are lost!

CHEVIOT: I disagree with you; I should say you are found.

BELVAWNEY: This man is a reckless fire-eater; he is jealous of me. He will assuredly shoot us both if he sees us here together. I am no coward – but I confess I am uneasy.

MISS TREHERNE (*to* CHEVIOT): Oh, sir, you have a ready wit; help us out of this difficulty, and we will both bless you—

BELVAWNEY: With our latest breath!

CHEVIOT: That decides me. Madam, remain here with me. Belvawney, withdraw.

(BELVAWNEY *retires.*)

I will deal with this maniac alone. All I ask is that, if I find it necessary to make a statement that is not consistent with strict truth, you, madam, will unhesitatingly endorse it.

MISS TREHERNE: I will stake my very existence on its veracity, whatever it may be.

CHEVIOT: Good. He is at hand. Belvawney, go.

(*Exit* BELVAWNEY.)

Now, madam, repose upon my shoulders, place your arms around me so – is that comfortable?

MISS TREHERNE: It is luxurious.

CHEVIOT: Good.

MISS TREHERNE: You are sure it does not inconvenience you?

CHEVIOT: Not at all. Go back – I like it. Now we are ready for him.

(*Enter* MCGILLICUDDY *with two friends dressed as for a wedding, with white favours.* MCGILLICUDDY *has pistols. All greatly excited.*)

MCGILLICUDDY: Where is the villain? I'll swear he is concealed somewhere. Search every tree, every bush, every geranium. Ha! They are here. Perjured woman! I've found you at last.

MISS TREHERNE (*to* CHEVIOT): Save me!

(BELVAWNEY *appears at back, listening.*)

MCGILLICUDDY: Who is the unsightly scoundrel with whom you have flown — the unpleasant-looking scamp whom you have dared to prefer to me? Uncurl yourself from around the plain villain at once, unless you would share his fate.

(MAGGIE *and* ANGUS *appear from cottage.*)

MISS TREHERNE: Major, spare him!

CHEVIOT: Now, sir, perhaps you will be so good as to explain who the deuce you are, and what you want with this lady?

MCGILLICUDDY: I don't know who you may be, but I'm McGillicuddy. I am betrothed to this lady; we were to have been married this morning. I waited for her at the church from ten till four, then I began to get impatient.

CHEVIOT: I really think you must be labouring under some delusion.

MCGILLICUDDY: Delusion? Ha ha!

(*Two friends produce large wedding cake.*)

Here's the cake!

CHEVIOT: Still, I think there's a mistake somewhere. This lady is my wife.

MCGILLICUDDY: What! Belinda! Oh, Belinda! Tell me that this unattractive man lies; tell me that you are mine and only mine, now and for ever!

MISS TREHERNE: I cannot say that. This gentleman is my husband!

(MCGILLICUDDY *falls sobbing on seat;* BELVAWNEY *tears his hair in despair;* MAGGIE *sobs on* ANGUS' *shoulder.*)

ACT II

SCENE

Double drawing room in SYMPERSON'*s house. Indications that a wedding is about to take place. A plate of tarts and a bottle of wine on table.*

Enter MINNIE SYMPERSON, *in wedding dress, followed by* PARKER, *her maid, holding her train.*

MINNIE: Take care, Parker – that's right. There! How do I look?

PARKER: Beautiful, miss; quite beautiful.

MINNIE (*earnestly*): Oh, Parker, am I really beautiful? Really, *really* beautiful, you know?

PARKER: Oh, miss, there's no question about it. Oh, I do so hope you and Mr Cheviot Hill will be happy.

MINNIE: Oh, I'm sure we shall, Parker. He has often told me that I am the tree upon which the fruit of his heart is growing; and one couldn't wish to be more than *that*. And he tells me that his greatest happiness is to see me happy. So it will be my duty – my *duty*, Parker – to devote my life, my whole life, to making myself as happy as I possibly can.

(*Enter* SYMPERSON, *dressed for wedding.*)

SYMPERSON: So, my little lamb is ready for the sacrifice. You can go, Parker. And I am to lose my pet at last; my little dicky bird is to be married today! Well, well, it's for her good. I must try and bear it – I must try and bear it.

MINNIE: And as my dear old papa comes into £1000 a year by it, I hope he won't allow it to distress him too much. He must try and bear up. He mustn't fret.

SYMPERSON: My child, I will not deny that £1000 a year is a consolation. It's quite a fortune. I hardly know what I shall do with it.

MINNIE: I think, dear Papa, you will spend a good deal of it on brandy, and a good deal more on billiards, and a good deal more on betting.

SYMPERSON: It may be so – I don't say it won't. We shall see, Minnie, we shall see. These simple pleasures would certainly tend to soothe your poor old father's declining years. And my darling has not done badly either, has she?

MINNIE: No, dear Papa – only, fancy! Cheviot has £2000 a year from shares in the Royal Indestructible Bank.

SYMPERSON: And don't spend £200. By the by, I'm sorry that my little bird has not contrived to induce him to settle anything on her; that, I think, was remiss in my tomtit.*

MINNIE: Dear Papa, Cheviot is the very soul of honour; he's a fine, noble, manly, spirited fellow, but if he *has* a fault, it is that he is very, oh very, *very* stingy. He would rather lose his heart's blood than part with a shilling unnecessarily. He's a noble fellow, but he's like that.

40

SYMPERSON: Still, I can't help feeling that if my robin had worked him judiciously—

MINNIE: Papa, dear, Cheviot is an all but perfect character – the very type of knightly chivalry – but he *has* faults, and, among other things, he's one of the worst tempered men I ever met in all my little life. Poor simple little Minnie thought the matter over very carefully in her silly, childish way, and she came to the conclusion, in her foolish little noddle, that, on the whole, perhaps she could work it better after marriage than before.

SYMPERSON: Well, well, perhaps my wren is right. (*Rises.*)

MINNIE: Don't laugh at my silly little thoughts, dear Papa, when I say I'm sure she is.

SYMPERSON: Minnie, my dear daughter, take a father's advice – the last he will ever be entitled to give you. If you would be truly happy in the married state, be sure you have your own way in everything. Brook no contradictions. Never yield to outside pressure. Give in to no argument. Admit no appeal. However wrong you may be, maintain a firm, resolute and determined front. These were your angel mother's principles through life, and she was a happy woman indeed. I neglected those principles, and while she lived I was a miserable wretch.

MINNIE: Papa dear, I have thought over the matter very carefully in my little baby noddle, and I have come to the conclusion – don't laugh at me, dear Papa – that it is my duty – my *duty* – to fall in with Cheviot's views in everything *before* marriage, and Cheviot's duty to fall into my views in everything *after* marriage. I think that is only fair, don't you?

SYMPERSON: Yes, I dare say it will come to that.

MINNIE: Don't think me a very silly little goose when I say I'm sure it will. Quite, quite sure, dear Papa. Quite. (*Exit.*)

SYMPERSON: Dear child – dear child! I sometimes fancy I can see traces of her angel mother's disposition in her. Yes, I think – I *think* she will be happy. But poor Cheviot! Oh, Lor', poor Cheviot! Dear me, it won't bear thinking of!

(*Enter* MISS TREHERNE, *unobserved. She is dressed in stately and funereal black.*)

MISS TREHERNE: Come here, manservant. Approach. I'm not going to bite you. Can I see the fair young thing they call Minnie Symperson?

SYMPERSON: Well really, I can hardly say. There's nothing wrong, I hope?

MISS TREHERNE: Nothing wrong? Oh, thoughtless, frivolous, light-hearted creature! Oh, reckless old butterfly! Nothing wrong! You've eyes in your head, a nose on your face, ears on each side of it, a brain of some sort in your skull, haven't you, butler?

SYMPERSON: Undoubtedly, but I beg to observe I'm not the—

MISS TREHERNE: Have you or have you not the gift of simple apprehension? Can you or can you not draw conclusions? Go to, go to – you offend me.

SYMPERSON (*aside*): There *is* something wrong, and it's
here. (*Touching his forehead.*) —I'll tell her you're here.
Whom shall I say?

MISS TREHERNE: Say that one on whose devoted head
the black sorrows of a long lifetime have fallen, even
as a funeral pall, craves a minute's interview with a
dear old friend. Do you think you can recollect that
message, butler?

SYMPERSON: I'll try, but I beg, I *beg* to observe, I'm not
the butler. (*Aside.*) This is a most surprising young
person! (*Exit.*)

MISS TREHERNE: At last I'm in my darling's home, the
home of the bright blithe carolling thing that lit, as
with a ray of heaven's sunlight, the murky gloom of
my miserable schooldays. But what do I see? Tarts?
Ginger wine? There are rejoicings of some kind
afoot. Alas, I am out of place here. What have I in
common with tarts? Oh, I am ill-attuned to scenes of
revelry! (*Takes a tart and eats it.*)

(*Enter* MINNIE.)

MINNIE: Belinda!

(*They rush to each other's arms.*)

MISS TREHERNE (*eating the tart all this time*): Minnie! My
own long-lost lamb! This is the first gleam of joy
that has lighted my darksome course this many and
many a day! And in spite of the change that time and
misery have brought upon me, you knew me at once!

43

MINNIE: Oh, I felt sure it was you from the message.

MISS TREHERNE: How wondrously fair you have grown! And this dress! Why, it is surely a bridal dress! Those tarts – that wine! Surely this is not your wedding day?

MINNIE: Yes, dear, I shall be married in half an hour.

MISS TREHERNE: Oh, strange chance! Oh, unheard-of coincidence! Married! And to whom?

MINNIE: Oh, to the dearest love – my cousin, Mr Cheviot Hill. Perhaps you know the name?

MISS TREHERNE: I have heard of the Cheviot Hills somewhere. Happy – strangely happy girl! You, at least, know your husband's name.

MINNIE: Oh yes, it's on all his pocket handkerchiefs.

MISS TREHERNE: It is much to know. I do not know mine.

MINNIE: Have you forgotten it?

MISS TREHERNE: No, I never knew it. It is a dark mystery. It may not be unfathomed. It is buried in the fathomless gulf of the eternal past. There let it lie.

MINNIE: Oh, tell me all about it, dear.

MISS TREHERNE: It is a lurid tale. Three months since I fled from a hated one, who was to have married me. He pursued me. I confided my distress to a young and wealthy stranger. Acting on his advice, I declared myself to be his wife; he declared himself to be my husband. We were parted immediately afterwards, and we have never met since. But this took place in Scotland; and by the law of that remarkable country we are man and wife, though I didn't know it at the time.

MINNIE: What fun!

MISS TREHERNE: Fun! Say rather, horror – distraction – chaos! I am rent with conflicting doubts! Perhaps he was already married; in that case, I am a bigamist. Maybe he is dead; in that case, I am a widow. Maybe he is alive; in that case I am a wife. What am I? Am I single? Am I married? Am I a widow? Can I marry? Have I married? May I marry? Who am I? Where am I? What am I? What is my name? What is my condition in life? If I am married, to whom am I married? If I am a widow, how came I to be a widow, and whose widow came I to be? Why am I his widow? What did he die of? Did he leave me anything? If anything, how much, and is it saddled with conditions? Can I marry again without forfeiting it? Have I a mother-in-law? Have I a family of stepchildren, and, if so, how many, and what are their ages, sexes, sizes, names and dispositions? These are questions that rack me night and day, and until they are settled, peace and I are not on terms!

MINNIE: Poor dear thing!

MISS TREHERNE: But enough of my selfish sorrows.

(Goes up to table and takes a tart. MINNIE *is annoyed at this.)*

Tell me about the noble boy who is about to make you his. Has he any dross?

MINNIE: I don't know. (*Secretly removes tarts to another table close to door.*) I never thought of asking – I'm such a goose. But Papa knows.

MISS TREHERNE (*eating*): Have those base and servile things called settlements been satisfactorily adjusted?*

MINNIE: I don't know. It never occurred to me to enquire. But Papa can tell you.

MISS TREHERNE: The same artless little soul!

MINNIE (*standing so as to conceal tarts from* MISS TREHERNE): Yes, I am quite artless – quite, quite artless. But now that you *are* here, you will stay and see me married.

MISS TREHERNE: I would willingly be a witness to my darling's joy, but this attire is, perhaps, scarcely in harmony with a scene of revelry.

MINNIE: Well, dear, you're not a cheerful object, and that's the truth.

MISS TREHERNE: And yet these charnel house rags* may serve to remind the thoughtless banquetters that they are but mortal.

MINNIE: I don't think it will be necessary to do that, dear. Papa's sherry will make *that* quite clear to them.

MISS TREHERNE: Then I will hie me home, and array me in garments of less sombre hue.

MINNIE: I think it would be better, dear. Those are the very things for a funeral, but this is a wedding.

MISS TREHERNE: I see very little difference between them. But it shall be as you wish, though I have worn nothing but black since my miserable marriage. There is breakfast, I suppose?

MINNIE: Yes, at dear Cheviot's house.

MISS TREHERNE: That is well. I shall return in time for it. Thank heaven I can still eat!

(*Takes a tart from table and exits, followed by* MINNIE. *Enter* CHEVIOT HILL. *He is dressed as for a wedding.*)

CHEVIOT: Here I am at last – quite flurried and hot after the usual row with the cabman, just when I wanted to be particularly calm and self-contained. I got the best of it, though. Dear me, this is a great day for me – a great day. Where's Minnie, I wonder? Arraying herself for the sacrifice, no doubt. Poof! This is a very nervous occasion. I wonder if I'm taking a prudent step. Marriage is a very risky thing; it's like Chancery* – once in it you can't get out of it, and the costs are enormous. There you are – fixed. Fifty years hence, if we're both alive, there we shall both be – fixed. That's the devil of it. It's an unreasonably long time to be responsible for another person's expenses. I don't see the use of making it for as long as that. It seems greedy to take up half a century of another person's attention. Besides, one never knows – one might come across somebody else one liked better – that uncommonly nice girl I met in Scotland, for instance. No, no, I shall be true to my Minnie – quite true. I am quite determined that nothing shall shake my constancy to Minnie.

(*Enter* PARKER.)

What a devilish pretty girl!

PARKER (*aside*): He's a mean young man, but he ought to be good for half a crown today.

CHEVIOT: Come here, my dear; a— How do I look?

PARKER: Very nice indeed, sir.

CHEVIOT: What, really?

PARKER: Really.

CHEVIOT: What, tempting, eh?

PARKER: Very tempting indeed.

CHEVIOT: Ha! The married state is an enviable state, Parker.

PARKER: *Is* it, sir? I hope it may be. It depends.

CHEVIOT: What do you mean by 'it depends'? You're a member of the Church of England, I trust? Then don't you know that in saying 'it depends' you are flying in the face of the marriage service? Don't go and throw cold water on the married state, Parker. I know what you're going to say – it's expensive. So it is, at first, very expensive, but with economy you soon retrench that. By a beautiful provision of Nature, what's enough for one is enough for two. This phenomenon points directly to the married state as our natural state.

PARKER: Oh, for that matter, sir, a tigress would get on with you. You're so liberal, so gentle, so – there's only one word for it – dovelike.

CHEVIOT: What, you've remarked that, eh? Ha ha! But dovelike as I am, Parker, in some respects, yet (*getting his arm round her*) in other respects... (*aside:*) deuced pretty girl! —in other respects I am a man, Parker, of a strangely impetuous and headstrong nature. I don't beat about the bush; I come quickly to the point. Shall I tell you a secret? There's something about you – I don't know what it is – that, in other words, you are the tree upon which— (*Aside:*) No, no, damn it, Cheviot – not today, not today!

PARKER: What a way you have with you, sir!

CHEVIOT: What, you've noticed that, have you? Ha ha! Yes, I have a way, no doubt; it's been remarked before.

Whenever I see a pretty girl (and you are a very pretty girl) I can't help putting my arm like that (*putting it round her waist*). Now, pleasant as this sort of thing is – and you find it pleasant, don't you?

(PARKER *nods.*)

Yes, you find it pleasant – pleasant as it is, it is decidedly wrong.

PARKER: It is decidedly wrong in a married man.

CHEVIOT: It is decidedly wrong in a married man. In a married man it's abominable, and I shall be a married man in half an hour. So, Parker, it will become necessary to conquer this tendency, to struggle with it and subdue it – in half an hour. (*Getting more affectionate:*) Not that there's any real harm in putting your arm round a girl's waist. Highly respectable people do it when they waltz.

PARKER: Yes, sir, but then a band's playing.

CHEVIOT: True, and when a band's playing it don't matter, but when a band is *not* playing, why it's dangerous, you see. You begin with this, and you go on from one thing to another, getting more and more affectionate, until you reach *this* stage (*kissing her*). Not that there's any real harm in kissing, either; for you see fathers and mothers, who ought to set a good example, kissing their children every day.

PARKER: Lor', sir, kissing's nothing; everybody does that.

CHEVIOT: That is your experience, is it? It tallies with my own. Take it that I am your father, you are my daughter – or take it even that I am merely your husband, and you my wife, and it would be expected of me. (*Kissing her.*)

PARKER: But I'm not your wife, sir.

CHEVIOT: No, not yet, that's very true, and, of course, makes a difference. That's why I say I must subdue this tendency; I must struggle with it; I must conquer it – in half an hour.

MINNIE (*without*): Parker, where's Mr Cheviot?

CHEVIOT: There is your mistress, my dear – she's coming. Will you excuse me? (*Releasing her.*) Thank you. Good day, Parker.

PARKER (*disgusted*): Not so much as a shilling; and that man's worth thousands!

(*Exit* PARKER. *Enter* MINNIE.)

CHEVIOT: My darling Minnie – my own, own To Come! (*Kissing her.*)

MINNIE: Oh, you mustn't crush me, Cheviot – you'll spoil my dress. How do you like it?

CHEVIOT: It's lovely. It's a beautiful material.

MINNIE: Yes; dear Papa's been going it.

CHEVIOT: Oh, but you're indebted to me for that beautiful dress.

MINNIE: To you! Oh, thank you – thank you!

CHEVIOT: Yes. I said to your papa, 'Now do for once let the girl have a nice dress; be liberal; buy the very best that money will procure – you'll never miss it.' So, thanks to me, he bought you a beauty. Seventeen and six a yard if it's a penny. Dear me! To think that in half an hour this magnificent dress will be *my* property!

MINNIE: Yes. Dear Papa said that as you had offered to give the breakfast at your house, he would give me the best dress that money could procure.

CHEVIOT: Yes − I *did* offer to provide the breakfast in a reckless moment; that's so like me. It was a rash offer, but I've made it, and I've stuck to it. Oh, then there's the cake.

MINNIE: Oh, tell me all about the cake.

CHEVIOT: It's a very pretty cake. Very little cake is eaten at a wedding breakfast, so I've ordered what's known in the trade as the three-quarter article.

MINNIE: I see − three-quarters cake, and the rest wood.

CHEVIOT: No − three-quarters wood, the rest cake. Be sure, my dear, you don't cut into the wood, for it has to be returned to the pastrycook to be filled up with cake for another occasion. I thought at first of ordering a seven-eighths article, but one isn't married every day − it's only once a year— I mean, it's only now and then. So I said, 'Hang the expense! Let's do the thing well.' And so it's a three-quarters.

MINNIE: How good you are to me! We shall be very happy, shall we not?

CHEVIOT: I − I hope so, yes. I *hope* so. Playfully happy, like two little kittens.

MINNIE: That will be delightful.

CHEVIOT: Economically happy, like two sensible people.

MINNIE: Oh, we must be very economical.

CHEVIOT: No vulgar display; no pandering to a jaded appetite. A refined and economical elegance; that is what we must aim at. A simple mutton chop, nicely broiled, for you; and *two* simple mutton chops, *very* nicely broiled, for me—

MINNIE: And some floury* potatoes—

CHEVIOT: A loaf of nice household bread—

MINNIE: A stick of celery—

CHEVIOT: And a bit of cheese, and you've a dinner fit for a monarch.

MINNIE: Then how shall we spend our evenings?

CHEVIOT: We'll have pleasant little fireside games. Are you fond of fireside games?

MINNIE: Oh, they're great fun.

CHEVIOT: Then we'll play at tailoring.

MINNIE: Tailoring? I don't think I know that game.

CHEVIOT: It's a very good game. You shall be the clever little jobbing tailor, and I'll be the particular customer who brings his own materials to be made up. You shall take my measure, cut out the cloth (real cloth, you know), stitch it together and try it on; and then I'll find fault like a real customer, and you shall alter it until it fits, and when it fits beautifully that counts one to you.

MINNIE: Delightful!

CHEVIOT: Then there's another little fireside game which is great fun. We each take a bit of paper and a pencil and try who can jot down the nicest dinner for ninepence, and the next day we have it.

MINNIE: Oh, Cheviot, what a paradise you hold open to me!

CHEVIOT: Yes. How's Papa?

MINNIE: He's very well and very happy. He's going to increase his establishment on the strength of the £1000 a year, and keep a manservant.

CHEVIOT: I know. I've been looking after some servants for him; they'll be here in the course of the morning. A cook, a housemaid and a footman. I found them through an advertisement. They're country people, and will come very cheap.

MINNIE: How kind and thoughtful you are! Oh, Cheviot, I'm a very lucky girl! (*Exit.*)

CHEVIOT: Yes, I think so too, if I can only repress my tendency to think of that tall girl I met in Scotland! Cheviot, my boy, you must make an effort; you are going to be married, and the tall girl is nothing to you!

(*Enter* PARKER.)

PARKER: Please, sir, here's a gentleman to see you.

CHEVIOT: Oh, my solicitor, no doubt. Show him up.

PARKER: And please, some persons have called to see you about an advertisement.

CHEVIOT: Oh, Symperson's servants. To be sure. Show up the gentleman, and tell the others to wait.

(*Exit* PARKER. *Enter* BELVAWNEY. *He looks very miserable.*)

CHEVIOT: Belvawney! (*Much confused.*) This is unexpected.

BELVAWNEY: Yes, Cheviot. At last we meet. Don't, oh don't, frown upon a heartbroken wretch.

CHEVIOT: Belvawney, I don't want to hurt your feelings, but I will not disguise from you that, not having seen you for three months, I was in hopes that I had got rid of you for ever.

BELVAWNEY: Oh, Cheviot, don't say that – I am so unhappy. And you have it in your power to make me comfortable. Do this, and I will bless you with my latest breath!

CHEVIOT: It is a tempting offer; I am not proof against it. We all have our price, and that is mine. Proceed.

BELVAWNEY: Miss Treherne – Belinda – whom I love so dearly, won't have anything to say to me.

CHEVIOT: It does her credit. She's a very superior girl.

BELVAWNEY: It's all through you, Cheviot. She declares that the mutual declaration you made to protect her from McGillicuddy amounts to a Scotch marriage.

CHEVIOT: What!!!

BELVAWNEY: She declares she is your wife. She professes to love me as fondly as ever; but a stern sense of duty to you forbids her to hold any communication with me.

CHEVIOT: Oh, but this is absurd, you know!

BELVAWNEY: Of course it is; but what's to be done? You left with Symperson immediately after making the declaration. As soon as she found you were gone she implored me to tell her your name and address. Of course I refused, and she quitted me, telling me that she would devote her life to finding you out.

CHEVIOT (*aside*): But this is simple madness. I can't have it! This day, too, of all others! If she'd claimed me last week, or even yesterday, I wouldn't have minded, for she's a devilish fine woman, but if she were to turn up now...! —Belvawney, my dear friend, tell me what to do – I'll do anything.

BELVAWNEY: It seems that there's some doubt whether this cottage, which is just on the border, is in England or Scotland. If it is in England, she has no case; if it is in Scotland, I'm afraid she has. I've written to the owner of the property to ascertain, and if, in the mean time, she claims you, you must absolutely decline to recognise this marriage for a moment.

CHEVIOT: Not for one moment!

BELVAWNEY: It was a mere artifice to enable her to escape from McGillicuddy.

CHEVIOT: Nothing more!

BELVAWNEY: It's monstrous – perfectly monstrous – that that should constitute a marriage. It's disgraceful – it's abominable. Damme, Cheviot, it's immoral.

CHEVIOT: So it is – it's immoral. That settles it in *my* mind. It's immoral.

BELVAWNEY: You're quite sure you'll be resolute, Cheviot?

CHEVIOT: Resolute? I should think so! Why, hang it all, man, I'm going to be married in twenty minutes to Minnie Symperson!

BELVAWNEY: What!

CHEVIOT (*confused at having let this out*): Didn't I tell you? I believe you're right; I did *not* tell you. It escaped me. Oh, yes, this is my wedding day.

BELVAWNEY: Cheviot, you're joking – you don't mean this! Why, I shall lose £1000 a year by it – every penny I have in the world! Oh, it can't be – it's nonsense!

CHEVIOT: What do you mean by 'nonsense'? The married state is an honourable estate, I believe? A man is not looked upon as utterly lost to all sense of decency because he's got married, I'm given to understand?

People have been married before this, and have not been irretrievably tabooed in consequence, unless I'm grossly misinformed? Then what the dickens do you mean by saying 'nonsense' when I tell you that I'm going to be married?

BELVAWNEY: Cheviot, be careful how you take this step. Beware how you involve an innocent and helpless girl in social destruction.

CHEVIOT: What do you mean, sir?

BELVAWNEY: You cannot marry; you are a married man.

CHEVIOT: Come, come, Belvawney, this is trifling.

BELVAWNEY: You are married to Miss Treherne. I was present, and can depose to the fact.

CHEVIOT: Oh, you're not serious.

BELVAWNEY: Never more serious in my life.

CHEVIOT: But, as you very properly said just now, it was a mere artifice – we didn't mean anything. It would be monstrous to regard that as a marriage. Damme, Belvawney, it would be immoral!

BELVAWNEY: I may deplore the state of the law, but I cannot stand tamely by and see it deliberately violated before my eyes.

CHEVIOT (*wildly*): But, Belvawney, my dear friend, reflect; everything is prepared for my marriage, at a great expense. I love Minnie deeply, devotedly. She is the actual tree upon which the fruit of my heart is growing. There's no mistake about it. She is my own To Come. I love her madly – rapturously. (*Going on his knees to* BELVAWNEY.) I have prepared a wedding breakfast at a great expense to do her honour. I have ordered four flys for the wedding party. I have taken two second-class Cook's tourists' tickets* for Ilfracombe, Devon, Exeter, Cornwall, Westward Ho! and Bideford Bay. The whole thing has cost me some twenty or twenty-five pounds, and all this will be wasted – utterly wasted – if you interfere. Oh, Belvawney, dear Belvawney, let the recollection of our long and dear friendship operate to prevent your shipwrecking my future life. (*Sobbing hysterically.*)

BELVAWNEY: I have a duty to do. I must do it.

CHEVIOT: But reflect, dear Belvawney; if I am married to Miss Treherne, you lose your income as much as if I married Minnie Symperson.

BELVAWNEY: No doubt, if you could prove your marriage to Miss Treherne. (*With melodramatic intensity:*) But you can't—

CHEVIOT: Those eyes!

BELVAWNEY (*with fiendish exultation*): You don't know where she is—

CHEVIOT: Oh, those eyes!

BELVAWNEY: The cottage has been pulled down, and the cottagers have emigrated to Patagonia—

CHEVIOT: Oh, those eyes!

BELVAWNEY: I'm the only witness left. *I* can prove your marriage if I like; but you can't. (*With satanic laugh:*) Ha ha ha ha! It's a most painful and unfortunate situation for you, and believe me, dear Cheviot, you have my deepest and most respectful sympathy. (*Exit.*)

CHEVIOT: This is appalling – simply appalling! The cup of happiness dashed from my lips just as I was about to drink a lifelong draught. The ladder kicked from under my feet just as I was about to pick the fruit of my heart from the tree upon which it has been growing so long. I'm a married man! More than that – my honeymoon's past, and I never knew it! Stop a moment, though. The bride can't be found, the cottage is pulled down and the cottagers have emigrated... what proof is there that such a marriage ever took place? There's only Belvawney, and Belvawney isn't a proof. Corroborated by the three cottagers, his word might be worth something; uncorroborated, it is worthless. I'll risk it. He can do nothing: the bride is nowhere, the cottagers are in Patagonia and—

(At this moment MRS MACFARLANE, MAGGIE *and* ANGUS *appear at the back. They stand bobbing and curtsying in rustic fashion to* CHEVIOT, *whom they do not recognise. He stares aghast at them for a moment, then staggers back to sofa.)*

CHEVIOT: The man, the woman and the girl, by all that's infernal!

MRS MACFARLANE *(producing paper)*: Gude day, sir. We've just ca'd to see ye about the advertisement.

CHEVIOT: I don't know you – I don't know you! Go away. *(Buries his head in a newspaper and pretends to read on sofa.)*

MAGGIE: Ah, sir, ye said that we were to ca' on ye this day at eleven o'clock, and sae we've coom a' the way fra Dumfries to see ye.

CHEVIOT: I tell you I don't know you. Go away. I'm not at all well. I'm very ill, and it's infectious.

ANGUS: We fear no illness, sir. This is Mistress Macfarlane, the gude auld mither, who'll cook the brose and boil the parritch, and sit wi' ye, and nurse ye through your illness till the sad day ye dee! (*Wiping his eye.*)

(CHEVIOT *pokes a hole with his finger through newspaper, and reconnoitres unobserved.*)

MRS MACFARLANE: And this is Meg, my ain lass Meg!

CHEVIOT (*aside*): Attractive girl, very. I remember her perfectly.

MRS MACFARLANE: And this is Angus Macalister, who's going to marry her, and who'll be mair than a son to me!

ANGUS: Oh, Mither, Mither, dinna say it, for ye bring the tear drop to my ee; an' it's no canny for a strong man to be blithering and soughing like a poor weak lassie! (*Wiping his eye.*)

(ANGUS *and* MRS MACFARLANE *sit.* MAGGIE *advances to hole in newspaper and peeps through.*)

MAGGIE: Oh, Mither, Mither! (*Staggers back into* ANGUS' *arms.*)

MRS MACFARLANE: What is it, Meg?

ANGUS: Meg, my weel lo'ed Meg, my wee wifie that is to be, tell me what's wrang wi' ee?

MAGGIE: Oh, Mither, it's him − the noble gentleman I plighted my troth to three weary months agone! The gallant Englishman who gave Angus twa golden pound to give me up!

ANGUS: It's the coward Sassenach who well nigh broke our Meg's heart!

MRS MACFARLANE: My lass, my lass, dinna greet – maybe he'll marry ye yet.

CHEVIOT (*desperately*): Here's another! Does anybody else want to marry me? Don't be shy! (*To* MRS MACFARLANE:) You, ma'am, *you're* a fine woman – perhaps *you* would like to try your luck?

MAGGIE: Ah, sir! I dinna ken your name, but your bonnie face has lived in my twa een, sleeping and waking, three weary, weary months! Oh, sir, ye should na' ha' deceived a trusting, simple Lowland lassie. 'Twas na' weel done – 'twas na' weel done! (*Weeping on his shoulder; he puts his arm round her waist.*)

CHEVIOT (*softening*): My good girl, what do you wish me to do? I remember you now perfectly. I *did* admire you very much – in fact, I do still; you're a very charming girl. Let us talk this over, calmly and quietly.

(MAGGIE *moves away.*)

No, you needn't go; you can stop there if you like. There, there, my dear! Don't fret. (*Aside*:) She *is* a very charming girl. I almost wish I – I really begin to think I – no, no! Damn it, Cheviot, not today!

MAGGIE: Oh! Mither, he told me he loved me!

CHEVIOT: So I did. The fact is, when I fell in love with you – don't go, my pretty bird – I quite forgot that I was engaged. There, there! I thought at the time that you were the tree upon which the fruit of my heart was growing, but I was mistaken. Don't go – you needn't go on that account. It was another tree—

MAGGIE (*weeping on* CHEVIOT*'s shoulder*): Oh, Mither, it
    was anither tree!

MRS MACFARLANE (*weeping on* ANGUS*' shoulder*): Angus,
    it was anither tree!

ANGUS: Dinna, Mither, dinna; I canna bear it! (*Weeps.*)

CHEVIOT: Yes, it was another tree — you can remain there
    for the present — in point of fact, it was growing on
    both trees. I don't know how it is, but it seems to grow
    on a great many trees — a perfect orchard — and you
    are one of them, my dear. Come, come, don't fret,
    you are one of them!

(*Enter* MINNIE *and* SYMPERSON.)

MINNIE: Cheviot!

SYMPERSON: What is all this?

CHEVIOT (*rapidly referring to a piece of paper given to him by*
    MRS MACFARLANE, *as if going over a washerwoman's*
    bill): 'Twenty-four pairs socks, two shirts, thirty-seven
    collars, one sheet, forty-four nightshirts, twenty-two
    flannel waistcoats, one white tie.' Ridiculous — quite
    ridiculous — I won't pay it.

MINNIE: Cheviot, who is this person who was found
    hanging on your neck? Say she is somebody — for
    instance, your sister or your aunt. Oh, Cheviot, say
    she is your aunt, I implore you!

(*The three cottagers curtsy and bow to* MINNIE.)

SYMPERSON: Cheviot, say she is your aunt, I command
    you.

CHEVIOT: Oh, I beg your pardon. I didn't see you. These ladies are… are my washerwomen. Allow me to introduce them. They have come… they have come for their small account.

(MAGGIE, *who has been sobbing through this, throws herself hysterically on to* CHEVIOT's *bosom.*)

There's a discrepancy in the items – twenty-two flannel waistcoats are ridiculous, and, in short, some washerwomen are like this when they're contradicted; they can't help it – it's something in the suds – it undermines their constitution.

SYMPERSON (*sternly*): Cheviot, I should like to believe you, but it seems scarcely credible.

MAGGIE: Oh, sir, he's na telling ye truly. I'm the puir Lowland lassie that he stole the hairt out of three months ago, and promised to marry; and I love him sae weel – sae weel – and now he's married to anither!

CHEVIOT: Nothing of the kind. I—

SYMPERSON: You are mistaken, and so is your mith— mother. He is not yet married to anith— nother.

MAGGIE: Why, sir, it took place before my very ain eyes, before us a', to a beautiful lady, three months since.

MINNIE: Cheviot, say that this is not true. Say that the beautiful lady was somebody – for instance, your aunt. Oh, say she was your aunt, I implore you!

SYMPERSON (*sternly*): Cheviot, say she was your aunt, I command you!

CHEVIOT: Minnie, Symperson, don't believe them – it was no marriage. I don't even know the lady's name

– I never saw her before, I've never seen her since. It's ridiculous – I couldn't have married her without knowing it – it's out of the question!

SYMPERSON: Cheviot, let's know exactly where we are. I don't much care whom you marry, so that you marry someone – that's enough for me. But please be explicit, for this is business, and mustn't be trifled with. Tell me all about it.

CHEVIOT (*in despair*): I cannot!

(*Enter* BELVAWNEY.)

BELVAWNEY: I can.

SYMPERSON: Belvawney!

BELVAWNEY: I was present when Cheviot and a certain lady declared themselves to be man and wife. This took place in a cottage on the Border – in the presence of these worthy people.

SYMPERSON: That's enough for me. It's a Scotch marriage! Minnie, my child, we must find you someone else. Cheviot's married. Belvawney, I am sorry to say, I deprive you of your income.

BELVAWNEY: I beg your pardon, not yet.

SYMPERSON: Why not?

BELVAWNEY: In the first place, it's not certain whether the cottage was in England or in Scotland; in the second place, the bride can't be found.

SYMPERSON: But she *shall* be found. What is her name?

BELVAWNEY: That I decline to state.

SYMPERSON: But you shall be made to state. I insist upon knowing the young lady's name.

(*Enter* MISS TREHERNE, *in a light and cheerful dress.*)

BELVAWNEY (*amazed*): Belinda Treherne!

MISS TREHERNE (*rushing to* MINNIE): Minnie, my own
old friend!

CHEVIOT: 'Tis she!

MISS TREHERNE (*turns and recognises* CHEVIOT): My
husband!

CHEVIOT: My wife!

(MISS TREHERNE *throws herself at* CHEVIOT'*s feet, kissing
his hands rapturously.* BELVAWNEY *staggers back.* MINNIE
faints in her father's arms. MAGGIE *sobs on* ANGUS' *breast.*)

ACT III

SCENE

Same as Act II. BELVAWNEY *discovered with* MISS TREHERNE *and* MINNIE. *He is singing to them.* MISS TREHERNE *is leaning romantically on piano.* MINNIE *is seated on a stool.*

BELVAWNEY (*sings*):

Says the old Obadiah to the young Obadiah,

I am drier, Obadiah, I am drier.*

CHORUS: I am drier.

BELVAWNEY:

Says the young Obadiah to the old Obadiah,

I'm on fire, Obadiah, I'm on fire.

CHORUS: I'm on fire.

MINNIE: Oh, thank you, Mr Belvawney. How sweetly pretty that is. Where can I get it?

MISS TREHERNE: How marvellous is the power of melody over the soul that is fretted and harassed by anxiety and doubt. I can understand how valuable must have been the troubadours of old, in the troublous times of anarchy. Your song has soothed me, sir.

BELVAWNEY: I am indeed glad to think that I have comforted you a little, dear ladies.

MINNIE: Dear Mr Belvawney, I don't know what we should have done without you. What with your sweet songs, your amusing riddles and your clever conjuring tricks, the weary days of waiting have passed like a delightful dream.

MISS TREHERNE: It is impossible to be dull in the society of one who can charm the soul with plaintive ballads one moment, and the next roll a rabbit and a guinea pig into one.

BELVAWNEY: You make me indeed happy, dear ladies. But my joy will be of brief duration, for Cheviot may return at any moment with the news that the fatal cottage was in Scotland, and then... Oh, Belinda, what is to become of me?

MISS TREHERNE: How many issues depend on that momentous question? Has Belvawney a thousand a year, or is he ruined? Has your father that convenient addition to his income, or has he not? May Maggie marry Angus, or will her claim on Cheviot be satisfied? Are you to be his cherished bride, or are you destined to a life of solitary maidenhood? Am I Cheviot's honoured wife, or am I but a broken-hearted and desolate spinster? Who can tell! Who can tell! (*Crosses to* MINNIE.)

BELVAWNEY (*goes to window in second drawing room*): Here is a cab with luggage – it is Cheviot! He has returned with the news! Ladies, one word before I go. One of you will be claimed by Cheviot – that is very clear. To that one (whichever it may be) I do not address myself – but to the other (whichever it may be) I say, I love you (whichever you are) with a fervour which I cannot describe in words. If you (whichever you are) will consent to cast your lot with mine, I will devote my life to proving that I love you and you only (whichever it may be) with a single-hearted and devoted passion, which precludes the possibility of my ever entertaining the slightest regard for any other woman in the whole world. I thought I would just mention it. Good morning! (*Exit.*)

MISS TREHERNE: How beautifully he expresses himself. He is indeed a rare and radiant being.

MINNIE (*nervously*): Oh, Belinda, the terrible moment is at hand.

MISS TREHERNE: Minnie, if dear Cheviot should prove to be my husband, swear to me that that will not prevent your coming to stop with us – with dear Cheviot and me – whenever you can.

MINNIE: Indeed I will. And if it should turn out that dear Cheviot is at liberty to marry me, promise me that that will not prevent you looking on our house – on dear Cheviot's and mine – as your home.

MISS TREHERNE: I swear it. We will be like dear, dear sisters.

(*Enter* CHEVIOT, *as from journey, with bag and rug.*)

MISS TREHERNE: Cheviot, tell me at once – are you my own... husband?

MINNIE: Cheviot, speak – is poor, little, simple Minnie to be your bride?

CHEVIOT: Minnie, the hope of my heart, my pet fruit tree! Belinda, my Past, my Present and my To Come! I have sorry news, sorry news.

MISS TREHERNE (*aside*): Sorry news! Then I am *not* his wife.

MINNIE (*aside*): Sorry news! Then she *is* his wife.

CHEVIOT: My dear girls, my very dear girls, my journey has been fruitless – I have no information.

MISS TREHERNE *and* MINNIE: No information!

CHEVIOT: None. The McQuibbigaskie* has gone abroad!

(*Both ladies fall weeping.*)

MISS TREHERNE: More weary waiting! More weary waiting!

MINNIE: Oh, my breaking heart! Oh, my poor bruised and breaking heart!

CHEVIOT: We must be patient, dear Belinda. Minnie, my own, we must be patient. After all, is the situation so very terrible? Each of you has an even chance of becoming my wife, and in the mean time I look upon myself as engaged to both of you. I shall make no distinction. I shall love you both, fondly, and you shall both love me. My affection shall be divided equally between you, and we will be as happy as three little birds.

MISS TREHERNE (*wiping her eyes*): You are very kind and thoughtful, dear Cheviot.

MINNIE: I believe, in my simple little way, that you are the very best man in the whole world!

CHEVIOT (*deprecatingly*): No, no.

MINNIE: Ah, but do let me think so: it makes me so happy to think so!

CHEVIOT: Does it? Well, well, be it so. Perhaps I am! And now tell me, how has the time passed since I left? Have my darlings been dull?

MISS TREHERNE: We should have been dull indeed but for the airy Belvawney. The sprightly creature has done his best to make the lagging hours fly. He is an entertaining rattlesnake – I should say, rattletrap.*

CHEVIOT (*jealous*): Oh, *is* he so? Belvawney has been making the hours fly, has he? I'll make *him* fly when I catch him!

MINNIE: His conjuring tricks are wonderful!

CHEVIOT: Confound his conjuring tricks!

MINNIE: Have you seen him bring a live hen, two hair brushes and a pound and a half of fresh butter out of his pocket handkerchief?

CHEVIOT: No, I have not had that advantage!

MISS TREHERNE: It is a thrilling sight.

CHEVIOT: So I should be disposed to imagine! Pretty goings on in my absence! You seem to forget that you two girls are engaged to be married to *me*!

MISS TREHERNE: Ah, Cheviot! Do not judge us harshly. We love you with a reckless fervour that thrills us to the very marrow – don't we, darling? But the hours crept heavily without you, and when, to lighten the gloom in which we were plunged, the kindly creature swallowed a live rabbit and brought it out, smothered in onions, from his left boot, we could not choose but smile. The good soul has promised to teach *me* the trick.

CHEVIOT: Has he? That's his confounded impudence. Now, once for all, I'll have nothing of this kind. One of you will be my wife, and until I know which, I will permit no Belvawneying of any kind whatever, or anything approaching thereto. When that is settled, the other may Belvawney until she is black in the face.

MISS TREHERNE: And how long have we to wait before we shall know which of us may begin Belvawneying?

CHEVIOT: I can't say. It may be some time. The McQuibbigaskie has gone to Central Africa. No post can reach him, and he will not return for six years.

MISS TREHERNE: Six years! Oh, I cannot wait six years! Why, in six years I shall be eight-and-twenty!

MINNIE: Six years! Why, in six years the Statute of Limitations* will come in, and he can renounce us both.

MISS TREHERNE: True – you are quite right. (*To* CHEVIOT:) Cheviot, I have loved you madly, desperately, as other woman never loved other man. This poor inexperienced child, who clings to me as the ivy clings to the oak, also loves you as woman never loved before. Even that poor cottage maiden, whose rustic heart you so recklessly enslaved, worships you with a devotion that has no parallel in the annals of the heart. In return for all this unalloyed affection, all we ask of you is that you will recommend us to a respectable solicitor.

CHEVIOT: But, my dear children, reflect – I can't marry all three. I am most willing to consider myself engaged to all three, and that's as much as the law will allow. You see, I do all I can. I'd marry all three of you with pleasure if I might; but, as our laws stand at present, I'm sorry to say − I'm very sorry to say − it's out of the question. (*Exit.*)

MISS TREHERNE: Poor fellow. He has my tenderest sympathy; but we have no alternative but to place ourselves under the protecting aegis of a jury of our countrymen!

(*Enter* SYMPERSON, *with two letters.*)

SYMPERSON: Minnie, Miss Treherne, the post has just brought me two letters − one of them bears a Marseilles postmark, and is, I doubt not, from the McQuibbigaskie! He must have written just before starting for Central Africa!

MINNIE: From the McQuibbigaskie? Oh, read, read!

MISS TREHERNE: Oh, sir! How can you torture us by this delay? Have you no curiosity?

SYMPERSON: Well, my dear, very little on this point − you see, it don't much matter to me whom Cheviot marries. So that he marries some one − that's enough for me. But, however, *your* anxiety is natural, and I will gratify it. (*Opens letter and reads:*) 'Sir, in reply to your letter, I have to inform you that Evan Cottage is certainly in England. The deeds relating to the property place this beyond all question.'

MINNIE: In England!

MISS TREHERNE (*sinking into a chair*): This blow is indeed a crusher. Against such a blow I cannot stand up! (*Faints.*)

MINNIE (*on her knees*): My poor Belinda – my darling sister – love! Oh, forgive me – oh, forgive me! Don't look like that! Speak to me, dearest – oh, speak to me – speak to me!

MISS TREHERNE (*suddenly springing up*): Speak to you? Yes, I'll speak to you! All is *not* yet lost! True, he is not married to me, but why should he not be? I am as young as you! I am as beautiful as you! I have more money than you! I will try – oh, how hard will I try!

MINNIE: Do, darling; and I wish – oh, how I wish you may get him!

MISS TREHERNE: Minnie, if you were not the dearest little friend I have in the world I could pinch you! (*Exit.*)

SYMPERSON (*who has been reading the other letter*): Dear me – how terrible!

MINNIE: What is terrible, dear Papa?

SYMPERSON: Belvawney writes to tell me the Indestructible Bank stopped payment yesterday, and Cheviot's shares are wastepaper.

MINNIE: Well, upon my word. There's an end of *him*!

SYMPERSON: An end of him. What do you mean? You are not going to throw him over?

MINNIE: Dear Papa, I am sorry to disappoint you, but unless your tomtit is very much mistaken, the Indestructible was not registered under the Joint-Stock Companies Act of Sixty-two,* and in that case the shareholders are jointly and severally liable to the whole extent of their available capital. Poor little Minnie don't pretend to have a business head, but she's not *quite* such a little donkey as *that*, dear Papa.

SYMPERSON: You decline to marry him? Do I hear rightly?

MINNIE: I don't know, Papa, whether your hearing is as good as it was, but from your excited manner, I should say you heard me perfectly. (*Exit.*)

SYMPERSON: This is a pretty business! Done out of a thousand a year, and by my own daughter! What a terrible thing is this incessant craving after money! Upon my word, some people seem to think that they're sent into the world for no other purpose but to acquire wealth, and, by Jove, they'll sacrifice their nearest and dearest relations to get it. It's most humiliating – most humiliating!

(*Enter* CHEVIOT, *in low spirits.*)

CHEVIOT (*throwing himself into a chair, sobbing aloud*): Oh! Uncle Symperson, have you heard the news?

SYMPERSON (*angrily*): Yes, I *have* heard the news; and a pretty man of business *you* are to invest all your property in an unregistered company!

CHEVIOT: Uncle, don't *you* turn against me! Belinda is not my wife! I'm a ruined man; and my darlings – my three darlings, whom I love with a fidelity, which, in these easygoing days, is simply quixotic – will have nothing to say to me. Minnie, your daughter, declines to accompany me to the altar. Belinda, I feel sure, will revert to Belvawney, and

Maggie is at this present moment hanging round that Scotch idiot's neck, although she knows that in doing so she simply tortures me. Symperson, I never loved three girls as I loved those three – never! Never! And now they'll all three slip through my fingers – I'm sure they will!

SYMPERSON: Pooh, pooh, sir. Do you think nobody loses but you? Why, I'm done out of a thousand a year by it.

CHEVIOT (*moodily*): For that matter, Symperson, I've a very vivid idea that you won't have to wait long for the money.

SYMPERSON: What d'you mean? Oh, of course, I understand.

CHEVIOT: Eh?

SYMPERSON: Mrs Macfarlane! I have thought of her myself. A very fine woman for her years – a majestic ruin, beautiful in decay. My dear boy, my very dear boy, I congratulate you.

CHEVIOT: Don't be absurd. I'm not going to marry anybody.

SYMPERSON: Eh? Why, then how——? I don't think I quite follow you.

CHEVIOT: There is another contingency on which you come into the money. My death.

SYMPERSON: To be sure! I never thought of that! And, as you say, a man can die but once.

CHEVIOT: I beg your pardon. I didn't say anything of the kind – you said it – but it's true, for all that.

SYMPERSON: I'm very sorry; but, of course, if you have made up your mind to it——

CHEVIOT: Why, when a man's lost everything, what has he to live for?

SYMPERSON: True, true. Nothing whatever. Still—

CHEVIOT: His money gone, his credit gone, the three girls he's engaged to gone.

SYMPERSON: I cannot deny it. It is a hopeless situation. Hopeless, quite hopeless.

CHEVIOT: His happiness wrecked, his hopes blighted; the three trees upon which the fruit of his heart was growing – all cut down. What is left but suicide?

SYMPERSON: True, true! You're quite right. Farewell. (*Going.*)

CHEVIOT: Symperson, you seem to think I *want* to kill myself. I don't want to do anything of the kind. I'd much rather live – upon my soul I would – if I could think of any reason for living. Symperson, can't you think of *something* to check the heroic impulse which is at this moment urging me to a tremendous act of self-destruction?

SYMPERSON: Something! Of course I can! Say that you throw yourself into the Serpentine – which is handy. Well, it's an easy way of going out of the world, I'm told – rather pleasant than otherwise, I believe – quite an agreeable sensation, I'm given to understand. But you – you get wet through; and your – your clothes are absolutely ruined!

CHEVIOT (*mournfully*): For that matter, I could take off my clothes before I went in.

SYMPERSON: True, so you could. I never thought of that. You could take them off before you go in – there's no reason why you shouldn't, if you do it in the dark – and *that* objection falls to the ground. Cheviot, my lion-hearted boy, it's impossible to resist your arguments – they are absolutely convincing. (*Shakes his hand. Exit.*)

CHEVIOT: Good fellow, Symperson – I like a man who's open to conviction! But it's no use – all my attractions are gone – and I can *not* live unless I feel I'm fascinating. Still, there's one chance left – Belinda! I haven't tried her. Perhaps, after all, she loved me for myself alone! It isn't likely – but it's barely possible.

(*Enter* BELVAWNEY, *who has overheard these words.*)

BELVAWNEY: Out of the question – you are too late! I represented to her that you are never likely to induce anyone to marry you now that you are penniless. She felt that my income was secure, and she gave me her hand and her heart.

CHEVIOT: Then all is lost; my last chance is gone, and the irrevocable die is cast! Be happy with her, Belvawney; be happy with her!

BELVAWNEY: Happy! You shall dine with us after our honeymoon and judge for yourself.

CHEVIOT: No, I shall not do that – long before you return I shall be beyond the reach of dinners.

BELVAWNEY: I understand – you are going abroad. Well, I don't think you could do better than try another country.

CHEVIOT (*tragically, drawing a pistol from his pocket*): Belvawney, I'm going to try another world!

BELVAWNEY (*alarmed*): What do you mean?

CHEVIOT: In two minutes I die!

BELVAWNEY: You're joking, of course?

CHEVIOT: Do I look like a man who jokes? Is my frame of mind one in which a man indulges in trivialities?

BELVAWNEY (*in great terror*): But my dear Cheviot, reflect—

CHEVIOT: Why should it concern you? You will be happy with Belinda. You will not be well off, but Symperson will, and I dare say he will give you a meal now and then. It will not be a nice meal, but still, it will be a meal.

BELVAWNEY: Cheviot, you mustn't do this; pray reflect; there are interests of magnitude depending on your existence.

CHEVIOT (*cocking the pistol*): My mind is made up.

BELVAWNEY (*wildly*): But I shall be ruined!

CHEVIOT: There is Belinda's fortune.

BELVAWNEY: She won't have me if I'm ruined! Dear Cheviot, don't do it – it's culpable – it's wrong!

CHEVIOT (*pointing the pistol to his head*): Life is valueless to me without Belinda.

BELVAWNEY (*desperately*): You shall have Belinda; she is much – very much – to me, but she is not everything. Your life is very dear to me; and when I think of our old friendship— Cheviot, you shall have anything you like, if you'll only consent to live!

CHEVIOT: If I thought you were in earnest; but no – no. (*Putting pistol to head.*)

BELVAWNEY: In earnest? of course I'm in earnest! Why, what's the use of Belinda to me if I'm ruined? Why, she wouldn't look at me.

CHEVIOT: But perhaps if I'm ruined, she wouldn't look at *me*.

BELVAWNEY: Cheviot, I'll confess all, if you'll only live. You – you are *not* ruined!

CHEVIOT: Not ruined?

BELVAWNEY: Not ruined. I – I invented the statement.

CHEVIOT (*in great delight*): You invented the statement? My dear friend! My very dear friend! I'm very much obliged to you! Oh, thank you, thank you a thousand times! Oh, Belvawney, you have made me very, very happy! (*Sobbing on his shoulder, then suddenly springing up.*) But what the devil did you mean by circulating such a report about me? How dare you do it, sir? Answer me that, sir.

BELVAWNEY: I did it to gain Belinda's love. I knew that the unselfish creature loved you for your wealth alone.

CHEVIOT: It was a liberty, sir, it was a liberty. To put it mildly, it was a liberty.

BELVAWNEY: It was. You're quite right – that's the word for it – it was a liberty. But I'll go and undeceive her at once. (*Exit.*)

CHEVIOT: Well, as I've recovered my fortune, and with it my tree, I'm about the happiest fellow in the world. My money, my mistress and my mistress' money, all my own. I believe I could go mad with joy!

(*Enter* SYMPERSON, *in deep black; he walks pensively, with a white handkerchief to his mouth.*)

CHEVIOT: What's the matter?

SYMPERSON: Hallo! You're still alive?

CHEVIOT: Alive? Yes. (*Noticing his dress:*) Why, is anything wrong?

SYMPERSON: No, no, my dear young friend, these clothes are symbolical; they represent my state of mind. After your terrible threat, which I cannot doubt you intend to put at once into execution—

CHEVIOT: My dear uncle, this is very touching; this unmans me. But, cheer up, dear old friend, I have good news for you.

SYMPERSON (*alarmed*): Good news? What do you mean?

CHEVIOT: I am about to remove the weight of sorrow which hangs so heavily at your heart. Resume your fancy check trousers – I have consented to live.

SYMPERSON: Consented to live? Why, sir, this is confounded trifling. I don't understand this line of conduct at all: you threaten to commit suicide; your friends are dreadfully shocked at first, but eventually their minds become reconciled to the prospect of losing you; they become resigned, even cheerful; and when they have brought themselves to this Christian state of mind, you coolly inform them that you have changed your mind and mean to live. It's not business, sir – it's not business.

CHEVIOT: But, my dear uncle, I've nothing to commit suicide for – I'm a rich man, and Belinda will, no doubt, accept me with joy and gratitude.

SYMPERSON: Belinda will do nothing of the kind. She has just left the house with Belvawney, in a cab, and under the most affectionate circumstances.

CHEVIOT (*alarmed*): Left with Belvawney? Where have they gone?

SYMPERSON: I don't know. Very likely to get married.

CHEVIOT: Married?

SYMPERSON: Yes, before the registrar.

CHEVIOT: I've been sold! I see that now! Belvawney has done me! But I'm not the kind of man who stands such treatment quietly. Belvawney has found his match. Symperson, they may get married, but they shall not be happy; I'll be revenged on them both before they're twenty-four hours older. She marries him because she thinks his income is secure. I'll show her she's wrong; I won't blow out my brains – I'll do worse.

SYMPERSON: What?

CHEVIOT: I'll marry.

SYMPERSON: Marry?

CHEVIOT: Anybody. I don't care who it is.

SYMPERSON: Will Minnie do?

CHEVIOT: Minnie will do – send her here.

SYMPERSON: In one moment, my dear boy – in one moment! (*Exit, hurriedly.*)

CHEVIOT: Belinda alone in a cab with Belvawney! It's maddening to think of it! He's got his arm round her waist at this moment, if I know anything of human nature! I can't stand it – I cannot and I will not stand it! (*Sits at writing table and prepares to write.*) I'll write at once to the registrar and tell him she's married. Oh, why am I constant by disposition? Why is it that when I love a girl I can think of no other girl but that girl, whereas, when a girl loves me she seems to entertain the same degree of affection for mankind at large? I'll never be constant again; henceforth I fascinate but to deceive!

(*Enter* MINNIE.)

MINNIE: Mr Cheviot Hill, Papa tells me that you wish to speak to me.

CHEVIOT (*hurriedly, writing at table*): I do. Miss Symperson, I have no time to beat about the bush; I must come to the point at once. You rejected me a short time since – I will not pretend that I am pleased with you for rejecting me – on the contrary, I think it was in the worst taste. However, let bygones be bygones. Unforeseen circumstances render it necessary that I should marry at once, and you'll do. An early answer will be esteemed, as this is business. (*Resumes his writing.*)

MINNIE: Mr Hill, dear Papa assures me that the report about the loss of your money is incorrect. I hope this may be the case, but I cannot forget that the information comes from dear Papa. Now, dear Papa is the best and dearest papa in the whole world, but he has a lively imagination, and when he wants to accomplish his purpose he does not hesitate to invent – I am not quite sure of the word, but I think it is 'bouncers'.

CHEVIOT (*writing*): You are quite right, the word is bouncers. Bouncers or bangers – either will do.

MINNIE: Then forgive my little silly fancies, Mr Hill; but, before I listen to your suggestion, I must have

83

the very clearest proof that your position is, in every way, fully assured.

CHEVIOT: Mercenary little donkey! I will not condescend to proof. I renounce her altogether. (*Rings bell.*)

(*Enter* MAGGIE *with* ANGUS *and* MRS MACFARLANE. ANGUS *has his arm round her waist.*)

CHEVIOT (*suddenly seeing her*): Maggie, come here. Angus, do take your arm from round that girl's waist. Stand back, and don't you listen. Maggie, three months ago I told you that I loved you passionately; today I tell you that I love you as passionately as ever; I may add that I am still a rich man. Can you oblige me with a postage stamp?

(MAGGIE *gives him a stamp from her pocket − he sticks it on to his letter.*)

What do you say? I must trouble you for an immediate answer, as this is not pleasure − it's business.

MAGGIE: Oh, sir, ye're ower late. Oh, Maister Cheviot, if I'd only kenned it before! Oh, sir, I love ye right weel; the bluid o' my hairt is nae sae dear to me as thou. (*Sobbing on his shoulder.*) Oh, Cheviot, my ain auld love! My ain auld love!

ANGUS (*aside*): Puir lassie, it just dra's the water from my ee to hear her. Oh, Mither, Mither! My hairt is just breaking. (*Sobs on* MRS MACFARLANE*'s shoulder.*)

CHEVIOT: But why is it too late? You say that you love me. I offer to marry you. My station in life is at least equal to your own. What is to prevent our union?

MAGGIE (*wiping her eyes*): Oh, sir, ye're unco guid to puir little Maggie, but ye're too late, for she's placed the matter in her solicitor's hands, and he tells her that an action for breach will just bring damages to the tune of a thousand pound. There's a laddie waiting outside noo, to serve the bonnie writ on ye! (*Turns affectionately to* ANGUS.)

CHEVIOT (*falling sobbing on to sofa*). No one will marry me. There is a curse upon me – a curse upon me. No one will marry me – no, not one!

MRS MACFARLANE: Dinna say that, sir. There's mony a woman – nae young, soft, foolish lassie, neither, but grown women o' sober age, who'd be mair a mither than a wife to ye; and that's what ye want, puir laddie, for ye're no equal to takin' care o' yersel'.

CHEVIOT: Mrs Macfarlane, you are right. I am a man of quick impulse. I see, I feel, I speak. I – you are the tree upon which – that is to say – no, no, d——n it, I can't; I can't! One must draw the line somewhere. (*Turning from her with disgust.*)

(*Enter* MISS TREHERNE *and* BELVAWNEY. *They are followed by* SYMPERSON *and* MINNIE.)

CHEVIOT: Belinda! Can I believe my eyes? You have returned to me – you have not gone off with Belvawney after all? Thank heaven, thank heaven!

MISS TREHERNE: I thought that, as I came in, I heard you say something about a tree.

CHEVIOT: You are right. As you entered I was remarking that I am a man of quick impulse. I see, I feel,

I speak. I have two thousand a year, and I love you passionately. I lay my hand, my heart and my income, all together, in one lot, at your feet!

MISS TREHERNE: Cheviot, I love you with an irresistible fervour that seems to parch my very existence. I love you as I never loved man before, and as I can never hope to love man again. But, in the belief that you were ruined, I went with my own adored Belvawney before the registrar, and that registrar has just made us one!

(MISS TREHERNE *turns affectionately to* BELVAWNEY, *who embraces her.*)

BELVAWNEY: Bless him for it – bless him for it!

CHEVIOT (*deadly calm*): One word. I have not yet seen the letter that blights my earthly hopes. For form's sake, I trust I may be permitted to cast my eye over that document? As a matter of business – that's all.

BELVAWNEY: Certainly. Here it is. You will find the situation of the cottage described in unmistakable terms. (*Hands the letter to* CHEVIOT.)

CHEVIOT (*reads*): 'In reply to your letter I have to inform you that Evan Cottage is certainly in England. The deeds relating to the property place this beyond all question.' Thank you – I am satisfied. (*Takes out pistol.*)

BELVAWNEY: Now, sir, perhaps you will kindly release that young lady. She is my wife!

(CHEVIOT's *arm has crept mechanically round* MISS TREHERNE's *waist.*)

MISS TREHERNE: Oh, Cheviot! kindly release me – I am his wife!

CHEVIOT: Crushed! Crushed! Crushed!

SYMPERSON (*looking over his shoulder at letter, reads*): 'Turn over.'

CHEVIOT (*despairingly*): Why should I? What good would it do? Oh! I see. I beg your pardon! (*Turns over the page.*) Halloa! (*Rises.*)

ALL: What?

CHEVIOT (*reads*): 'P.S. – I may add that the border line runs through the property. The cottage is undoubtedly in England, though the garden is in Scotland.'

MISS TREHERNE: And we were married in the garden!

CHEVIOT: Belinda, we were married in the garden!

(MISS TREHERNE *leaves* BELVAWNEY, *and turns affectionately to* CHEVIOT, *who embraces her.*)

BELVAWNEY: Belinda, stop a bit! Don't leave me like this!

MISS TREHERNE (*crosses to* BELVAWNEY): Belvawney, I love you with an intensity of devotion that I firmly believe will last while I live. But dear Cheviot is my husband now – he has a claim upon me which it would be impossible – nay, criminal – to resist. Farewell, Belvawney; Minnie may yet be yours!

(BELVAWNEY *turns, sobbing, to* MINNIE, *who comforts him;* MISS TREHERNE *crosses back to* CHEVIOT.)

Cheviot – my husband – my own old love – if the devotion of a lifetime can atone for the misery of the last few days, it is yours, with every wifely sentiment of pride, gratitude, admiration and love.

CHEVIOT (*embracing her*): My own! My own! Tender blossom of my budding hopes! Star of my life! Essence of happiness! Tree upon which the fruit of my heart is growing! My Past, my Present, my To Come!

PICTURE

(CHEVIOT *is embracing* MISS TREHERNE, BELVAWNEY *is being comforted by* MINNIE, ANGUS *is solacing* MAGGIE *and* MRS MACFARLANE *is reposing on* MR SYMPERSON'*s bosom.*)

NOTE ON THE TEXT

The text of this edition is based on that printed in Gilbert's *Original Plays: Second Series* (London: Chatto & Windus, 1881), which was supervised by Gilbert, and is essentially the same as the edition published by Samuel French (undated, but probably published in 1877), except for the excision of some small technical details, mostly concerning stage positioning (L., R., etc.). However, Gilbert's 'Note' and the note on 'Costumes' are taken from the Samuel French edition, which has also been consulted in the case of any doubtful readings in the *Original Plays* version. As was conventional at the time, many of the stage notes were given in the original text after the action they direct; in this edition they have been moved up to their conventional position in front of the directed action. Where stage notes indicate an aside, an em dash (—) has been used to demonstrate where the speaker ends the aside. In some cases, spelling and punctuation have been silently corrected to make the text more appealing to the modern reader.

NOTES

3   *CHEVIOT HILL*: The Cheviot Hills, also called the Cheviots, are a hill range straddling the Scottish border region.

3   *ANGUS MACALISTER*: Gilbert borrowed the name Angus MacAlister from a character in the 1866 drama *Ours* by his friend Thomas William ('T.W.') Robertson (1829–71). Comic novelist P.G. Wodehouse (1881–1975) was a great admirer of Gilbert's works, and devotees of his Blandings Castle saga will be immediately reminded of the Castle's irascible head gardener, Angus McAllister, who first appeared in *Leave it to Psmith* (1923).

3   *suit of dittos*: i.e. a suit made from one material, so that all parts match.

3   *glengarry*: A brimless, cleft hat with ribbons hanging from the back; forms part of Highland dress.

4   *snood*: A type of hairband historically worn by unmarried women in Scotland.

4   *Gretna*: Gretna Green is a village in Dumfriesshire, just within the Scottish border, historically famous as the destination for English and Welsh couples wishing to marry without their parents' consent. Following the passing of the Clandestine Marriages Act of 1753, the marriage in England or Wales of a person under the age of 21 was not valid without the consent of parents or guardians. However, the Act was not in force in

Scotland, so that Gretna Green, the first Scottish village on the main coach route from England, became a favourite destination for young eloping couples.

5 *24, The Boltons*: This address in South Kensington was Gilbert's residence from 1876 to 1883.

10 *Dumfries*: A town, formerly a royal burgh, in the historic county of Dumfriesshire in Scotland. Maggie appears to mean the whole of Dumfriesshire rather than the town of Dumfries itself, which lies about thirty miles away from the Scottish-English border.

11 *gillieing*: Acting as an attendant or guide on a hunting or fishing expedition.

11 *cot*: Cottage.

17 *Scotch marriage*: Following the Clandestine Marriages Act (see second note to p. 4), English couples wishing to marry without their parents' consent could travel to Scotland, where a difference in the marriage laws permitted the ceremony to take place. Further, under Scottish law, an irregular 'marriage by declaration', consisting simply of a mutual statement of marriage before witnesses, could be considered binding. However, the legal status of these so-called 'Scotch marriages' was not clear-cut; this uncertainty formed the basis of Wilkie Collins' 1870 novel *Man and Wife*, in which such a marriage may have taken place by accident. The Scottish marriage by declaration was finally abolished under the Marriage (Scotland) Act of 1939.

20 *remarked*: In the sense of 'noticed'.

21 *apostrophising*: An apostrophe is a speech addressed to an absent person or object.

22 *latest breath*: Last (dying) breath.

40   *tomtit*: Songbird; blue tit.

45   *settlements*: Elsewhere in *Engaged*, the word 'settlement'
      is used in a general sense, to refer to a financial arrange-
      ment (the income of £1000 a year which Belvawney
      receives as long as Cheviot Hill remains single). How-
      ever, here Belinda Treherne is referring specifically to
      the marriage settlement made by Symperson for his
      daughter Minnie's benefit. Historically, a woman's
      possessions became the property of her husband
      upon marriage. (This explains Cheviot's later exultant
      boast that 'in half-an-hour this magnificent [wedding]
      dress will be *my* property!') The situation started to
      change under the Married Women's Property Act of
      1870, which permitted a married woman's earnings
      to be treated as her own property, and a further Act
      in 1882 allowed a married woman to have complete
      personal control over all of her possessions. (These
      Acts applied in England, Wales and Ireland, but not
      Scotland.) However, *Engaged*, first published in 1877,
      was written before the 1882 Act. Marriage settlements
      were still common in well-to-do families: these were
      financial arrangements made before the marriage by
      the parents of the affianced couple, in order to provide
      an income for the wife during the marriage, and addi-
      tionally a 'jointure' for the widow and a 'portion' for
      any children after the father's death.

46   *charnel house rags*: A charnel house is a building or
      vault for dead bodies.

47   *Chancery*: The Court of Chancery was a historical
      Court of Equity in England and Wales, presided
      over by the Lord Chancellor, and dealing with civil

disputes. It had long been notorious for the slowness and high costs of its processes, as depicted in Dickens' *Bleak House* (1853). The Court ceased to exist in 1875, when its role was taken on by the Chancery Division of the newly created High Court of Justice of England and Wales.

52 *floury*: Spelt 'flowery' in the extant texts, which is evidently an error.

57 *Cook's tourists' tickets*: A reference to the tourist agency founded by Thomas Cook (1808–92).

67 *I am drier, Obadiah*: These lines are from the very popular 1876 comic song 'The Two Obadiahs' by Henry P. Lyste, originally sung by the comedian J.L. Toole (creator of the title role in Gilbert and Sullivan's *Thespis*) in his touring one-man show, *Spelling Bee*. Almost simultaneously, the song also appeared, with alternative lyrics by Robert Reece, in the burlesque *Young Rip Van Winkle*, where it was sung by Nellie Farren (who had created the role of Mercury in *Thespis*); but it is Lyste's original version that is quoted here. Billed as 'a moral song', it tells the sad tale of two men who decided to drink paraffin and light a smoke afterwards (see page 99, where the song is reproduced). By 1877, 'The Two Obadiahs' was everywhere, sung in burlesques and amateur concerts, played on barrel-organs and carolled by drunken revellers – altogether an unlikely choice of ballad to be sung romantically to one's sweethearts in a drawing room.

70 *The McQuibbigaskie*: Although this character is never formally introduced, we gradually infer that he is the owner of the cottage at the centre of the plot.

71 *rattletrap*: Chatterbox.

72 *Statute of Limitations*: A reference to legislature that prevents cases being brought after a certain amount of time has passed.

74 *the Joint-Stock Companies Act of Sixty-two*: The Companies Act 1862 was a piece of legislature that changed the nature of companies, largely relating to the limitations of liability.

A GLOSSARY OF

STAGE SCOTS

Engaged was never intended to be an accurate portrayal of real life. Instead, it takes and plays with the conventions of Victorian drama. This includes the depiction of three 'Lowland peasant' characters who speak not in any recognisable version of the Scots language, but in English spiced with a hotchpotch of Scots words, sometimes used inaccurately, and further seasoned with antique English formations such as 'I love thee dearly, as thou well knowest.' Their language might be called, for want of a better term, Stage Scots.

Much of their vocabulary is fairly self-explanatory: 'ye' for 'you', 'naething' for 'nothing', 'mither' for 'mother', etc. However, as the reader may find some other terms less easy to decipher, there follows a brief glossary of Stage Scots, interpreted in line with Gilbert's apparent intended meaning.

I am grateful for the invaluable assistance of J. Derrick McClure, editor of the W.S. Gilbert Society Journal and a well-known authority on the Scots language. Any errors are, of course, my own.

ANDREW CROWTHER

BAIRN	child, darling
BANNOCK	a flat cake, usually of oatmeal but also possibly of barley or pease-meal, or a mixture, baked on a girdle
BLITHERING	(more correctly 'blethering'): talking foolishly
BRAW	fine, good
BROSE	oatmeal stirred in boiling water or milk – differing from *parritch* in that it is not actually boiled in the liquid
EE	eye (plural: een; also used as 'you')
FASHT	angry, irritated
FRA	from
GIN	if
GREET	cry, weep
KEN	know
KIRK	church
MUCKLE	much
MUN	(more correctly 'maun'): must
OWER	very, excessively
PARRITCH	porridge
SAE	so
SAIR	sore; very
SASSENACH	English person (derogatory)
SIC	such
SOUGHING	sighing or moaning
UNCO	very, extremely

THE TWO OBADIAHS

A Moral Song

WORDS AND MUSIC BY HENRY P. LYSTE

I

Said the young Obadiah, to the old Obadiah,
  I am dry, Obadiah, I am dry,
Said the old Obadiah, to the young Obadiah,
  So am I, Obadiah, so am I.
But the two Obadiahs had between them not a *sou*,
Every Publican smiled and said, Oh ho! my friend, it's you?
May I ask, Obadiah, if you'll pay what is due,
  Said the two Obadiahs, O be d—d, O be d—d.

II

Said the young Obadiah, to the old Obadiah,
  I've a plan, Obadiah, I've a plan,
Said the old Obadiah, to the young Obadiah,
  If that's so, Obadiah, I'm your man!
Said the young Obadiah, For weak liquor don't repine,
For my Landlady's uncle sells a proper sort of wine,
It's in quarts, Obadiah, and it's called Paraffine,
  Said the old Obadiah, 'That'll do.'

III

Said the young Obadiah, to the old Obadiah,
 What a joke, Obadiah, what a joke!
Said the old Obadiah, to the young Obadiah,
 Let us smoke, Obadiah, let us smoke!
For I wouldn't hint for worlds that the liquor isn't right,
But it's potent, Obadiah, and I feel I'm getting tight,
So just hand me the baccabox and serve out a light,
 Obadiah, Obadeeah, Obaday.

IV

Said the young Obadiah, to the old Obadiah,
 I am drier, Obadiah, I am drier,
Said the old Obadiah, to the young Obadiah,
 I'm on fire, Obadiah, I'm on fire!
As the two Obadiahs were consumed by their thirst,
The neighbours hurried in and prevented the worst,
By pumping so hard that the engines all burst,
 Obadiah, Obadiah, didn't die!

MORAL

Said the old Obadiah, to the young Obadiah,
  A lesson, Obadiah, I have learnt!
Said the young Obadiah, to the old Obadiah,
  I am burnt, Obadiah, I am burnt!
And because, Obadiah, we did all but cremate,
In future we'll try to avoid such a fate,
Oh! smoking and drinking are sins very great,
  Said the old Obadiah, 'Stick to tea!'

MORE CLASSIC THEATRE FROM
RENARD PRESS

ISBN: 9781913724061
Paperback
£7.99 • 160pp

ISBN: 9781913724054
Paperback with gold foil
£7.99 • 128pp

ISBN: 9781913724368
Paperback with gold foil
£7.99 • 96pp

DISCOVER THE FULL COLLECTION AT
WWW.RENARDPRESS.COM